# When You Lose Someone You Love

Randy Petersen

Publications International, Ltd.

**Randy Petersen** is an author and church educator from New Jersey with more than 50 books to his credit, including *Red Letters* (Revell), *Bible Fun Stuff* (Tyndale House), and *Why Me, God?* (Publications International, Ltd.). A prolific creator of church curriculum, he's also a contributor to the *Quest Study Bible*, the *Revell Bible Dictionary*, and the iLumina Bible software. When not writing, Randy teaches public speaking at a community college.

**Image Credits**
**Cover Image:** Shutterstock
**Interior Images:** Adobe Image Library, Brand X, Corbis RF, Digital Vision, iStockphoto, Photodisc, Shutterstock, Thinkstock

**Acknowledgments**
All scripture quotations are taken from the New Revised Standard Version of the Bible. Copyright © 1989 National Council of the Churches of Christ in the United States of America. Used by permission. All rights reserved.

Copyright © 2012 Publications International, Ltd. All rights reserved. This book may not be reproduced or quoted in whole or in part by any means whatsoever without written permission from:

Louis Weber, CEO
Publications International, Ltd.
7373 North Cicero Avenue
Lincolnwood, Illinois 60712

Permission is never granted for commercial purposes.

ISBN-13: 978-1-4508-4578-6
ISBN-10: 1-4508-4578-9

Manufactured in China.

8 7 6 5 4 3 2 1

Library of Congress Control Number: 2011942587

# Contents

*Introduction*

# Losing Someone You Love

*In all human sorrows, nothing gives comfort but love and faith.*

—Leo Tolstoy, *Anna Karenina*

When you lose someone you love... it hurts. That might seem obvious, but we sometimes forget it. We try to soldier on, shrugging it off, getting back to business as quickly as possible. A personal loss shakes you, saps you. You feel pain in places you didn't know you had.

If you are reeling from the loss of a loved one, you're normal. If you find yourself crying all night, sleeping all day, or suddenly doing strange things—don't fret. It doesn't mean you're going crazy. It just means you've lost someone you really love.

There is no surefire formula, no pill that will magically "cure" you of your grief. Time heals. Faith helps. And the support of solid friends and family will get you through the worst of it. Still, there will always be a tender spot in your soul, a corner dedicated to the memory of the one you've lost. You might get back to normal in a year or so, but beyond that, you'll still shed an occasional tear. That is as it should be.

Over the millennia of human existence, people have observed the grieving process. The Greeks wrote epic poetry for their fallen heroes. King David wept bitterly over his rebellious son, "O my son Absalom, my son, my son Absalom! Would I had died instead of you, O Absalom, my son, my son!" (2 Samuel 18:33). The apostle Paul expressed Christian hope of the hereafter—"so that you may not grieve as others do who have no hope" (1 Thessalonians 4:13)—and yet Peter attended the tear-soaked funeral of a dear Christian woman (Acts 9:39).

Faith is not a shield, warding off the pain of loss. It is more like a prism through which we view the painful situation. People of faith still hurt. We still suffer denial, anger, depression, and the whole spectrum of human emotion—but for people of faith, the whole scene has a tint of hope and love.

Many believers routinely turn to the Bible for comfort in their times of deepest need, and this book will encourage you to do that. When you lose someone you love, you desperately need some encouraging words. You might need to be reassured of God's love for you and for the person you're mourning. You might need permission to experience the overwhelming grief. Above all, you might need a heavenly perspective on these matters. As God sees it, death is not the end. He has a glorious eternity prepared for us. We find great consolation in these scriptural truths.

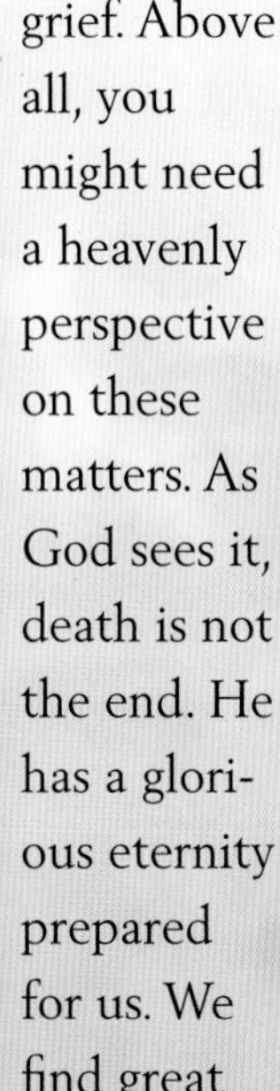

But there are different kinds of comfort—the gentle kind and the powerful kind.

The gentle kind of comfort takes the form of quickly quoted phrases and loving pats. Someone might say, “Don’t feel bad, because all things work together for good.” This is true and often much needed. People want to show their concern for you, and these consolations are lovely gifts.

But sometimes you need a deeper comfort. You don’t want to be told, “Don’t feel bad,” because you do feel bad, and you will for quite some time. What you need to hear is that God has not forgotten you, that he will embrace you in the most difficult times. You need to hear that you’ll get through this pain—not around it, but through it—and that a new day will dawn at the end of this dark night of the soul.

You need to know that it’s okay to cry. Hey, it’s okay to holler and throw things. The loss of a loved one affects your entire self—your mind, your emotions, your body, and your spirit. But you will recover, in the proper time. You will not always understand why your loved one was taken—you don't need to. You need to hear that your muddled feelings don't make you a bad person, a weak believer, or a traitor to the loved one who's gone.

The great thing about the Bible is that it's both gentle and powerful. It gives us great assurances, but it doesn't sugarcoat the message. It tells us the truth about God—that we won't always understand him, but we can receive his amazing love. "My ways [are] higher than your ways," he tells us (Isaiah 55:9). He is beyond us but also beside us.

Your path through grief is *your* path. It doesn't need to—and shouldn't—match anyone else's.

This book is organized around various "times" that you might experience in your grieving process. Some of these "times" match up to the classic stages of grief, but there are others that reflect different circumstances, concerns, or points along the journey. For instance, you might be grieving the expected loss of someone with a terminal illness. That situation is explored in the "Times of Uncertainty" chapter. Or you might have been stunned by the sudden loss of someone you expected to live much longer. In those situations, there's usually a state of shock that the mourner needs to deal with. That is discussed in the "Times of Sudden Shock" chapter.

While every chapter will have helpful insights (and supportive poems, verses, and prayers), they won't all pertain to your particular journey. So feel free to pick and choose which chapters to read. You might want to start by looking at the table of contents and circling chapter titles that seem to describe where you are right now. Read those chapters first, then go back and poke through the whole book in context. Or you might want to keep this book by your bedside over the next year and check back in at regular intervals. As your "times" change, you'll find yourself drawn to different chapters.

It is my hope and prayer that you will find this book

a valuable resource in this difficult period in your life, a tour guide of sorts in this strange land of grieving. Don't think of it as some professor who tells you what you "need to know" about the cold, calculated subject of bereavement. Think of it as a friend who engages in a conversation with you—consoling you, supporting you, challenging you—when you are ready.

**When we lose a loved one, we must take time to go within and reaffirm our connection with God. Once we are able to feel God's presence at work in our lives, we will know that we already have all we need to help us move beyond the grief and begin to live and love again.**

I pray that this book will be a source of both gentle and powerful comfort to you. It will not answer all your questions or even try to. I aim to tell you the truth about grieving: good, bad, and in between. And I want to open up the scriptures in a way that will reveal the message of divine power and love.

—Randy Petersen

*Chapter 1*

# Times of Uncertainty

## *When a loss is expected, feared, or presumed, how can you find solid ground to grieve on?*

*But I trust in you, O Lord;*
*I say, "You are my God."*
*My times are in your hand.*

—Psalm 31:14–15

# Moving Brings Life Changes

It was a big move for Bob and Irma. Having spent most of their adult lives on the East Coast, they were headed west to a retirement facility just down the road from where their oldest son lived. Their two other grown children were making the whole process easy for them—working with a realtor to sell their old house, arranging to haul some furniture cross-country, and selling other items.

"All you need to do is to hop on that plane," they told their folks.

But hopping wasn't so easy, especially after 80-year-old Irma hurt her back in a fall just a week before moving day. She did make the trip, but in considerable pain. The settling-in process was difficult, getting used to another bed, a different climate, and new doctors.

Throughout her life, Irma had dealt with various ailments—heart trouble in her youth, diabetes, even a bout with cancer. She had always been sickly yet durable. Even before the move, she had a shelf full of pills to take—blood thinner, blood-pressure meds, and others for pain. With the fall, and the move, and her new doctors, and the new living arrangements, her medications needed to be recalibrated. This was a painful and perilous process. Blood pressure spiked. Her heart skipped. Blood sugar soared for a time. A skin rash. Pneumonia. General lethargy.

It so happened that Irma was already in a hospital facility, being treated for diabetes, when a routine check discovered that she had heart failure. She survived that momentary crisis, but the doctor made it clear that this was the beginning of the end. At some point—in the next week, month, year, maybe decade, her heart would stop beating.

This sort of "death sentence" would be devastating for someone in her 30s. At 80, it's less of a shock, but it's still a shock. In the months since their move, Bob had been running him-

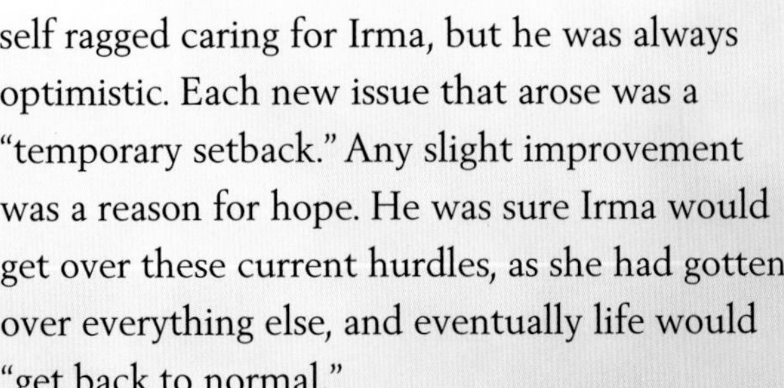

self ragged caring for Irma, but he was always optimistic. Each new issue that arose was a "temporary setback." Any slight improvement was a reason for hope. He was sure Irma would get over these current hurdles, as she had gotten over everything else, and eventually life would "get back to normal."

But this was the new normal.

Their oldest son was with them as they grilled their newest doctor for straight answers. This would not get better, they were told. At Irma's age, there was no medication or surgery that would fix it. She had an old, damaged heart, and it would most likely kill her. There was no timetable—maybe months, though they hoped for years.

Bob got a ride back to his apartment from his oldest son, who wanted to make sure he got the message. "You know she could die," the son said tenderly.

"Yes, I know."

A corner was turned in that moment. Instead of dodging the death issue, Bob and Irma began to embrace it. They enrolled in hospice care and were amazed at the cadre of helpers, counselors, and comforters who came to ease their lives in these final days. The other children were alerted, and they came to visit, each fearing that this might be their last time seeing their mother alive. The couple even began planning the funeral service together.

This difficult time also saw a deepening of their faith. They would pray together after dinner and even sing hymns. A devout Christian, Irma would be ready to meet her Maker, whenever that time came. Meanwhile, they were both thanking God for each day they had.

And so they waited.

Irma had good days and bad days. On her good days, which were surprisingly frequent, they would often take drives through the countryside, exploring this new territory. Other relatives came to pay their respects. The out-of-state children came back to say goodbye all over again.

> **Cast all your anxiety on him, because he cares for you.**
>
> **—1 Peter 5:7**

Months went by with no major turn for the worse. Hospice care was re-evaluated and re-upped. Normally their patients survive six months or less, but Irma was defying the odds. She was quite ready for death at this point, but apparently death wasn't ready for her. Bob tried to keep his hopes in check. He had to keep telling himself that the original prognosis was still in effect. Her heart problem wasn't going away—it was just forestalled for a time. He tried to live each day enjoying the gift of that day, but it was hard to keep from anticipating the sorrow he would soon feel.

"Are these months of knowing she could die at any time part of the grieving process?" Bob wrote to his kids.

The answer is yes. The grieving process starts whenever it needs to and continues as long as it has to. In a case like this, when a future loss is anticipated, it's common for loved ones to get a head start on it. We're not just grieving a death; we're grieving the pain and sorrow of that death—and those feelings start as soon as we hear the gloomy prognosis. So, yes, Bob has already begun to grieve. You may have recognized his denial in the early going, but once he recognized the seriousness of Irma's condition, he was ripe for the collection of emotions that accompanies the grieving process.

Perhaps you find yourself in a similar time of uncertainty. Does a loved one suffer from a terminal illness? You might already be grieving, even if your loved one is still with you. You're trying to enjoy each moment together, but you're also worried about the sorrow that will soon come.

Uncertainty changes the whole process significantly. When a loved one passes, you feel that sharp pain of loss. You might live in a stage of denial for a short time, "forgetting" what has happened, acting as if the person is still around, but you'll move through that. The trouble with uncertainty is that the grieving process gets stalled at the start, like a car idling in the driveway. The machinery of grief is whirring, but there's not much to grieve yet. You can't "get over" your sorrow because you haven't gotten *into* it yet.

*Lord, how can I endure this life of sorrows, unless you strengthen me with your mercy and grace? Do not turn your face from me. Do not withdraw your consolation from me, lest my soul become like a waterless desert. Teach me, O Lord, to do your will, and to live humbly. You alone know me perfectly, seeing into my soul. You alone can give lasting peace and joy.*

—Thomas à Kempis

Do not worry about anything, but in everything by prayer and supplication with thanksgiving let your requests be made known to God. And the peace of God, which surpasses all understanding, will guard your hearts and your minds in Christ Jesus.

—Philippians 4:6–7

Remember to turn to God for help, for in him there is rescue, refuge, and peace.

***I see a robin's egg hatching, Lord, and am set free from my doubts and fretting. For, while life is not always filled with joy and happiness, I know it is always held in your hand.***

# Dealing with Uncertainty

It's common for people in times of uncertainty to wander between denial and "dealing with it." They can pretend the loss will never really happen (as Bob was tempted to do on Irma's good days), or they can try to prepare themselves for the eventual loss.

Of course there are different kinds of uncertainty. Sometimes we're unsure of a diagnosis. A person is seriously ill, and the doctors don't know what's wrong. The ailment seems life threatening, and maybe it is, but no one fully knows. If they figure it out, maybe there's a cure. Maybe the patient can be up and running tomorrow. Or maybe there will be a funeral. We find ourselves at the mercy of experts, and if they're unsure, we don't know how to feel.

Sometimes we're unsure of the prognosis. In this case, the doctors know what's wrong, but they don't know how the patient will respond to treatment. They can give us a range of possibilities, but they can't say for certain what the outcome will be.

In such cases, medical staff will often give us numbers. "There's a 30 percent chance that the patient will pull through." At first that might seem cold and clinical. How can you reduce a person's life to a math problem? But that actually can help us emotionally, as we try to find a landing spot between denial and dealing. Those numbers, if we hear them correctly, can tell us how much hope we should have—and how seriously we should prepare for the worst.

**He gives power to the faint, and strengthens the powerless.**

**—Isaiah 40:29**

And often, as in Irma's case, we're unsure about timing. The doctors might have given an estimate—so many months to live—but that's just guesswork. We prepare ourselves for an impending loss, but we don't know when it will hit. Often there are partial losses along the way:

when the patient is unable to work anymore; when the patient goes into a hospital, leaving home for the last time; when the patient loses certain physical abilities—mobility, sight, or speech. Each of these losses is mourned as it happens, but everyone knows they're headed for a bigger loss ahead.

In the midst of these uncertainties, the friends and family of a dying person often face big decisions, and it's hard to be sure what choices to make. Is it better for someone to spend their final days at home, surrounded by familiar people and things, or in a nursing home or hospital, surrounded by professional care? At what point should the medical staff be instructed to let a patient go and to forego resuscitation? Sometimes there are experimental treatments that offer a long shot at survival, or at least some extension of life. There are questions about funerals and wills and cremation and organ donation.

These are all highly emotional decisions, made at a highly emotional time. How can you be sure about any decision?

*So you have pain now; but I will see you again, and your hearts will rejoice, and no one will take away your joy from you.*

—John 16:22

*Steer the ship of my life, good Lord, to your quiet harbor, where I can be safe from the storms of sin and conflict. Show me the course I should take. Renew in me the gift of discernment, so that I can always see the right direction in which I should go. And give me the strength and courage to choose the right course, even when the sea is rough and the waves are high, knowing that through enduring hardship and danger in your name we shall find comfort and peace.*

—Basil of Caesarea

# Baffling Uncertainty

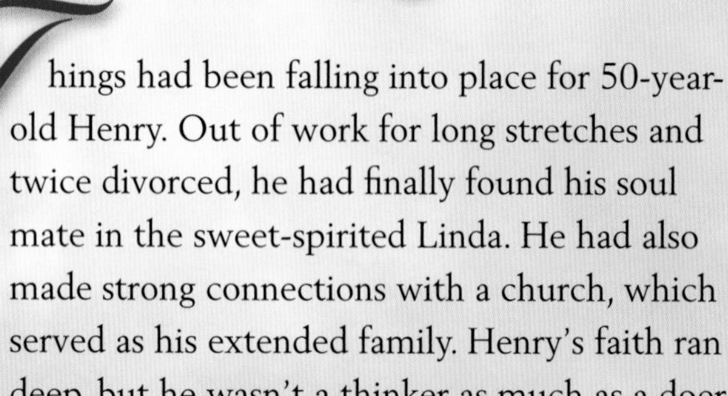

Things had been falling into place for 50-year-old Henry. Out of work for long stretches and twice divorced, he had finally found his soul mate in the sweet-spirited Linda. He had also made strong connections with a church, which served as his extended family. Henry's faith ran deep, but he wasn't a thinker as much as a doer. He'd be afraid to speak in public, but he would help out in any way he could.

The news was devastating when Henry was diagnosed with an advanced stage of cancer. The doctors gave him six months to live. His wife, Linda, rallied the prayer support of the church. Surely a miracle would occur. But Henry was getting sicker and sicker. It wasn't his style to ask for help, but he finally confided in some friends from the church, who did all they could to comfort both Henry and Linda in this trying time.

One such friend was Anita. Like Henry, she was a doer. She had no clue why God would let this happen, and she wasn't about to try to explain it, but she would *be there* when people needed her. In this uncertain time, Henry and Linda needed her.

One valuable thing she did was to listen to the doctors. Anita had relatives who were also doctors, and she would call them to double-check what Henry's doctors were saying. As much as Linda wanted to believe in a miracle, there were no signs of a healing here. Anita was sensitive but clear in her conversations with Henry's wife—she needed to prepare for his passing. When it was clear that a hospital could do nothing more for Henry, he wanted to spend his last days at home. Anita double-checked the facts and supported that decision. She was there with Linda

when Henry died and continued to support her in the following months.

Linda would tell you that Anita was a godsend. Oh, there were preachers from the church who offered care and counseling, but it was Anita who truly ministered to her in this time of deep sorrow. In her down-to-business way, Anita cut through the baffling uncertainty.

*Day by day and with each passing moment,*
*strength I find to meet my trials here;*
*trusting in my Father's wise bestowment,*
*I've no cause for worry or for fear.*
*He whose heart is kind beyond all measure*
*gives unto each day what he deems best—*
*lovingly, its part of pain or pleasure,*
*mingling toil with peace and rest.*

—Lina Sandell (translated by A. L. Skoog),
"Day by Day and with Each Passing Moment"

*Lord of joy,*

*Joy! Now there's a word I haven't considered for a while. Joy? Is that possible? After what I've been through, could I ever feel your sweet joy again? Survival, yes. Maintenance, sure. I'm already slogging through each day, and I thank you for that. But joy? What bonfire will you have to light in my heart to make that happen? I can't wait to see how you bring joy to my morning.*

*In humble faith, Amen.*

Blessings, like miracles, appear only when we believe in them. Faith gives us the eyes with which to see and the ability to believe what we are seeing.

# Ideas for Your Times of Uncertainty

***Get good help.*** Maybe you don't have a helper like Anita to sort through the uncertainties, but you might be able to find one. Think through your friends and relatives to see if there's someone who might fill this role. Consider the people who have said, "If there's anything I can do, let me know." Many of us close in upon ourselves in times of sorrow. We want to deal with suffering on our own. But in times of uncertainty, we need people beside us to help us hear, understand, plan, and cope. You're not looking for someone who will make decisions for you, but one who will take the time to understand the situation and talk with you about it.

So don't be afraid to ask someone to visit the doctor with you so you can compare notes after-

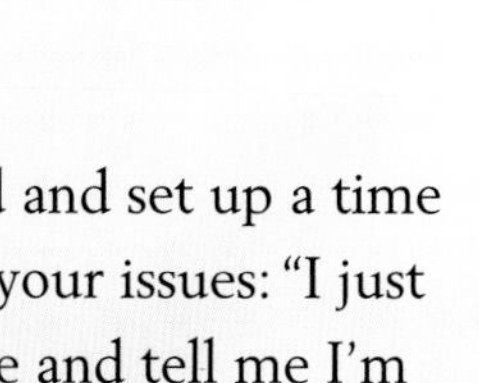

ward. You might call a friend and set up a time where you can talk through your issues: "I just need someone to listen to me and tell me I'm not crazy." Look for people who will be honest with you—in fact, you may need to give them explicit permission to tell you things that are hard to hear.

***Ask questions.*** Some doctors are very good about telling us what we need to know. Some aren't. The truth is, in times of crisis, we're not always very good at listening either. And sometimes we get shy about asking doctors to repeat or clarify—they're so busy, so smart, and so scientific, but that's their job. Don't be afraid to sound dumb. There's no such thing as a stupid question, especially when it concerns your health or a loved one's condition.

Understand that doctors are sometimes uncertain themselves. They might not be able to give you a clear diagnosis, a solid prognosis, or a reliable timetable. You might have to live with some scientific uncertainty, but make sure you have all the answers available to you. Don't grab only the most positive or the most negative possibility. Try to understand the full range of options.

***Help your loved one put affairs in order.*** It's hard enough to get past your own denial, but you might also have to challenge the denial of the loved one you're losing. It's not really helpful to push a best-case scenario if it's likely your loved one will die soon—especially if there's unfinished business to attend to. You don't need to quash all hope, but try to present a realistic picture. "You might get better, and we're praying for that, but what if you don't? Are you ready for that?"

Understand that this is also an emotionally charged time for your loved one, but try to help him or her focus on what needs to be done. It might help to make a list and prioritize the items. Is there a will? Does the family have all the financial information? Are there wishes regarding the funeral, burial, or cremation?

Beyond the business aspects, are there people who need to be seen, hatchets buried, forgiveness asked? Is there a "bucket list" of things to do before the person "kicks the bucket"? Skydiving might not be possible right now, but maybe there's some other goal that could be checked off the list.

***Give yourself a break.*** You might find that some of your own emotions shock you during this time. Some people find themselves growing impatient, as if they wish their loved one would hurry up and die so they can get on with the grieving. They don't really want that; it's just an idle thought they feel terrible about. Others might become emotionally distant from the dying loved one, fearing that growing closer in these final days would just mean more pain later.

**O God, help us not to despise or oppose what we do not understand.**

**—William Penn**

Emotions are unruly things. It's hard to police them. So, in this trying time, forgive yourself for inappropriate feelings that flash through your consciousness. These thoughts don't mean you're a bad person or that you don't love the person you're losing. They just reflect the emotional stress you're going through.

***Say what needs saying.*** Flash forward five years, long after this dear one has departed. Will there be anything you wish you had said? Well, this may be the last chance you have to say it.

Be careful about this. If there's anything extremely heavy (family secrets or past abuse), you might want to talk with a counselor or minister first. Unburdening yourself could put undue pressure on your loved one. You should also make this a matter of prayer. But maybe there's an apology you need to make or forgiveness you need to offer. Maybe you simply need to say, "I love you."

***Savor every moment.*** Try to forget your worries about what will happen *next,* and bring yourself back to *now.* You still have some moments to be together with this dear one. Take advantage of that opportunity. Celebrate life in laughter and silence, in loving words and lilting songs, in vivid sights and stirring sounds.

Mark was diagnosed with a lymphosarcoma and died five months later. After his passing, his 27-year-old wife wrote this to some friends: "One real cause for celebration for Mark during these last few months was not so much the knowledge that he would be mourned after he died, but the very real knowledge that he was loved while he lived. The time between January and May was for us a grace period, a gift—a chance to live deeply and openly with the knowledge of death, and to have made real to us the love and caring support of those around us."

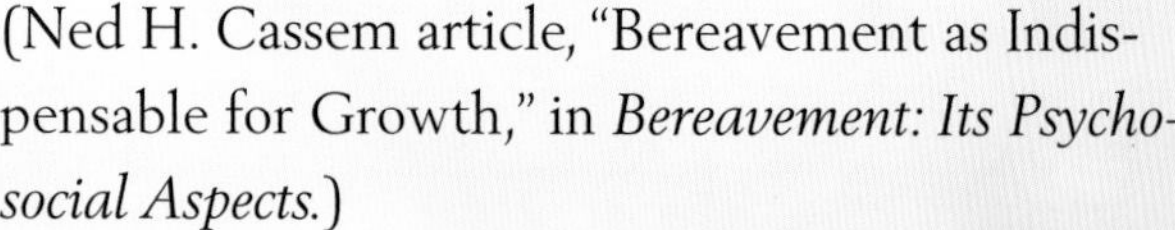

(Ned H. Cassem article, “Bereavement as Indispensable for Growth,” in *Bereavement: Its Psychosocial Aspects.*)

***Deepen your faith.*** There is something about the approach of death that invigorates the soul, almost as if the gates of heaven are already beginning to open. Often, with the nearness of the afterlife, “the things of earth grow strangely dim,” as an old song says. Sometimes dying people understand life more clearly than ever.

Not always. There are some who refuse to “go gently into that good night,” as the poet Dylan Thomas put it, who “rage against the dying of the light.” Some are beset by doubts and fears.

Either way, this is certainly a time to talk about issues of faith. It is a time to connect with the Creator as best you can—you and the dear one who is moving on. It is a time for prayer and praise, a time to thank the Lord for the gift of life and trust the Lord for what lies ahead—however uncertain that might be. As a saying has it, “We may not know what the future holds, but we know who holds the future.”

*Calm the waves of this heart, O God;*
*calm its tempests.*
*Calm yourself, O my soul, so that God is*
*able to rest in you, so that God's peace*
*may cover you.*
*Yes, You can give us peace, O God, peace*
*that the whole world can never take away.*

—Søren Kierkegaard

There is a sanctuary of peace within us that we can access anytime by doing a simple breathing meditation. We close our eyes and focus on our breath as it goes in and out of our body. We clear the mind of all turmoil, gently keeping our focus on the breath. In time, thoughts fade, and we begin to feel a sense of connectedness with a higher presence. We keep breathing, gently, quietly, and we touch the face of God.

Yet, in the maddening maze of things,
And tossed by storm and flood,
To one fixed trust my spirit clings;
I know that God is good!. . .
I know not where His islands lift
Their fronded palms in air;
I only know I cannot drift
Beyond His love and care.

—John Greenleaf Whittier, "The Eternal Goodness"

***Seeking courage, Lord, I bundle my fears and place them in your hands. Too heavy for me, too weighty even to ponder in this moment, such shadowy terrors shrink to size in my mind and—how wonderful!—wither to nothing in your grasp.***

*God hath not promised*
*Skies always blue,*
*Flower-strewn pathways*
*All our lives through;*
*God hath not promised*
*Sun without rain,*
*Joy without sorrow,*
*Peace without pain.*
*But God hath promised*
*Strength for the day.*
*Rest for the labor,*
*Light for the way,*
*Grace for the trials,*
*Help from above,*
*Unfailing sympathy,*
*Undying love.*

—Annie Johnson Flint

*Chapter 2*

# Times of Sudden Shock

***When death strikes suddenly, the heart and head can shut down for a time, and even when you think you're past it, there are aftershocks.***

My soul is bereft of peace; . . . The steadfast love of the LORD never ceases, his mercies never come to an end; they are new every morning; great is your faithfulness.

—Lamentations 3:17, 22–23

# Shocking Loss

You can write this story yourself. If it has happened to someone you love, the details are etched in your memory. A phone call in the middle of the night. A drunk driver. A freak accident. A stray bullet. A heart attack or stroke.

You're reading this chapter because you had some sort of sudden shock when a loved one died. You just weren't expecting it. They were too young, too healthy, too *alive*—and your world completely changed when they passed.

That experience is significantly different from a lingering illness, and your recovery will face unique challenges. These words may stir up some bad memories, and we want to be sensitive about that, but it's also important to understand what you've gone through.

The heart of the matter is this: *People aren't supposed to die.* This is especially true when they're young. We talk about those who are "cut short" in the "prime of life." There's something wrong about that. It bothers us.

But how young do people have to be? 40? 60? Nowadays people routinely live into their 90s, and even then their passing can seem sudden. So it's not just a matter of age. The shock of a sudden loss can affect us whether the person we're mourning was 8 or 80.

Simply put, we expect to keep living in a world where this dear one exists, and suddenly they are gone. That changes everything.

Any loss is a tragedy, whether expected or not. We grieve deeply even when we've had months or years to prepare. We ride a range of emotions—debilitating sorrow, energizing anger, gnawing guilt, and so on. But a sudden loss compresses all of those emotions, putting greater pressure on us. It's not just a roller-coaster ride; it's a bucking bronco. It overloads our circuitry. Some of us shut down key parts of our personality. Others take the wild ride, bouncing from one emotion to another. The trauma of a sudden loss can bury itself deep within our psyche. It can inhabit dreams, incite fantasies, create obsessions, and sometimes it can reoccur years after the event happened.

You might think you're going crazy, but in most cases it's just the normal processing of an extraordinary event. (We do, however, recommend that you get professional help if you're feeling desperate. Even if your responses are quite normal, a good counselor can guide you through the healing process.)

**He will wipe every tear from their eyes. Death will be no more; mourning and crying and pain will be no more, for the first things have passed away.**

**—Revelation 21:4**

When someone has fair warning that a loved one is about to die, certain steps can be taken to prepare for that loss—words spoken, questions answered, papers signed. But a sudden loss leaves many important details unaddressed. There is no closure. Loose strings are everywhere—emotionally and practically. Often the survivors find it hard to *begin* the grieving process because they're still dealing with the paperwork.

*He heals the brokenhearted, and binds up their wounds.*

—Psalm 147:3

When the sudden loss of someone we dearly love brings a cold darkness to our lives, it seems that darkness will be forever with us and our hearts will never feel joy again. We believe then that night will never end and day will never come. Yet the darkness will leave and the night will end when we hold on to our Lord, for he will bring light back into our lives. And in that light, our hopes will be renewed.

The best thing about the future is that it comes only one day at a time.

—Abraham Lincoln

# Dealing with the "Uns"

The experience of grieving a sudden loss is often shaped by an assortment of "uns": unfinished business, unanswered questions, unresolved anger, uncontrolled emotions.

## Unfinished business

A sudden death leaves many things unsaid. Think about all that people routinely put off saying or doing.

- "One of these days I'll teach you how to change the oil."
- "I should tell you about your grandpa."
- "I really need to make a will."

There are grudges held and forgivenesses withheld. There are stories to be told and wisdom to unfold. There are cryptic PIN numbers and hidden addictions and family secrets. And do we ever tell people enough how much we love them?

An unexpected tragedy calls the bluff on our unfinished business. It imposes a new deadline we never saw coming. The survivors are left in a half-constructed world, as if they're trying to complete a jigsaw puzzle with pieces missing. This often creates an unsettled feeling, a tension. Life feels suddenly incomplete, and there's little you can do about it.

***Relational.*** Jane and her mom got along well, but there was a wall between them that stretched back for decades. When Jane was a teenager, working through the normal confusion of adolescence, her overly emotional mom had meddled too much. Whatever victory or defeat Jane experienced, whatever joy or sorrow, whatever loving or longing—Mom was there to feel it for her. Jane wasn't always sure how to feel about things, and Mom interpreted this as an unhealthy blockage of normal emotions. "It's okay to cry," Mom would say, but Jane didn't always *want* to cry. She felt her emotional life being co-opted by her well-meaning mother, and so, as a survival technique, she began to withdraw, to keep secrets, to stop telling her mother anything. She knew her mom noticed this and was hurt by it, but she was desperate to reclaim her own life.

Now Jane was in her 40s and Mom was in her 70s, and those issues were ancient history. In therapy, Jane had worked through some of this. Her counselor agreed that her teenage withdrawal was a pretty good stratagem, given the circumstances, and it might have saved her from a destructive rebellion later on.

Still, Jane thought it might be helpful to talk it over with her mother, to try to tear down the wall that had kept her safe in those tender years, to heal old hurts and find a new level of intimacy. She just didn't know how to bring it up.

Then her mother had a stroke and was gone. Everyone was comforting Jane, saying that her mother had lived a good, long life, but Jane knew it wasn't long enough. She had unfinished relational business with her mom that had never gotten done. And now it never would.

This sort of thing is very common. People often regret the things they *didn't* say when their loved ones were alive.

- "I love you."
- "I'm sorry; forgive me."
- "Thank you."
- "Remember that thing you thought? You were right."
- "You really messed up my life."
- "I know you did what you thought best."
- "I forgive you."

Like Jane, we often avoid saying these things because they're hard to say. We might fear that it's counterproductive to unearth long-buried problems. Jane had a decent relationship with her mom, though it wasn't as close as it could have been. Why should she risk alienating her mom entirely? That reasoning keeps a lot of people from having difficult conversations—and they might be right! But that doesn't stave off their regrets when that loved one has passed.

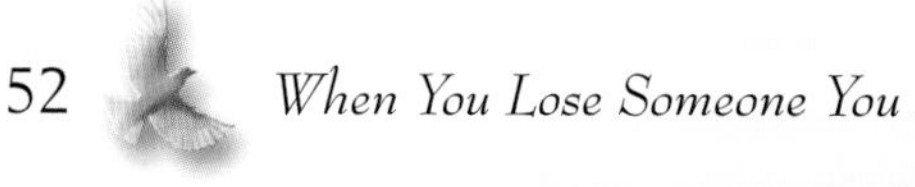

***Spiritual.*** Many Christians worry about the spiritual standing of a loved one who has passed on. If the person has never professed faith in Christ, that would certainly be considered unfinished *spiritual* business. This is often one of those conversations that people intend to have but never quite get around to. A terminal illness can get those conversations going, and there have been many "deathbed conversions." But in the case of sudden death, that option isn't available. As a result, the survivors grieve all the more, uncertain of their loved one's spiritual destiny.

We should emphasize the word *uncertain*. While some have adopted a systematic interpretation of the Bible that would insist on eternal doom for any who have not uttered certain words of faith, the Bible also assures us that God doesn't want anyone to "perish" eternally (2 Peter 3:9, KJV). This gives us hope in these uncertain situations. Some have suggested that there's a moment between death and the afterlife when God gives a person one more chance to trust him. Perhaps in such a moment a person might gather all the memories of words spoken and love shown—maybe even *your* words and actions—and finally says yes to God's overwhelming love. We simply don't know.

***Practical.*** Losing a loved one suddenly usually means loose ends—some important, some not. It can be very frustrating, in your moment of deepest grief, to deal with the minutiae of life: car keys, credit cards, DVDs to return, pets to feed.

In addition, a death creates a whole new layer of practical considerations—funeral arrangements, burial, organ donation, the will, sometimes issues with a hospital or ER, with police or coroner. These practical matters distract us from our grief, and at the same time they keep reminding us of our loss.

**Unanswered questions**

The first question is generally *How?* Followed quickly by *Why?* Medical examiners can usually pinpoint a cause of death, but the reason is often more elusive. *Why didn't she wear her seatbelt? Why would a healthy person suddenly have a heart attack?*

Often the questions revolve around some of the relational or spiritual issues we've just discussed. *What did he think about God, or about me?* In the case of suicide, another set of agonizing questions arises: *What would lead this dear person to that tragic choice?*

We also wonder about the experience of death. *Was there pain? Was there fear? Was there faith?*

## Unresolved anger

Anger is an unwanted guest at a funeral. It seems inappropriate in a time of grief, especially shared grief, but we find plenty of reasons to be irked, and it tends to surface at odd times. One problem with anger is its lack of precision. You get angry at one person or situation, and it sprays out to everyone. (This can then provoke angry reactions from others, which make you angrier.)

***You're angry at anyone who caused or abetted the death.*** Words cannot describe the wrath of parents toward the drunk driver who killed their child. They have every right to be angry, and we can only bless and admire those who use this passion for better purposes. But the blame is not always this clearly located. You might be angry at a doctor who made a bad diagnosis (you think); or at your daughter-in-law, who allowed your son to smoke and gain weight; or at the city, for failing to put a guard rail at that dangerous curve.

***You're angry at yourself for not doing more to help.*** Sometimes we can identify specific things we could have done to prevent the death or perhaps to make the person's life easier beforehand. We often overestimate what we could have done and thus berate ourselves too much.

***You're angry at the person who died.*** This is often very hard to admit, but it's very common. The funeral tends to focus on the best attributes of the dearly departed. What's there to be angry about? Well, he smoked and drank, she ate too many potato chips, he never saw a doctor, she drove recklessly, etc. We can often find behaviors that led, in some way, to death. But anger doesn't always need to define a reason; sometimes it just springs from a feeling of abandonment. *How could you leave me?*

***You're angry at God.*** This too is difficult to admit, and the issues reverberate through our spiritual lives. Many people get mad at God but never own up to that feeling. As a result, they put up a wall. God becomes the aloof great-uncle they only see on holidays. And they lose access to their main source of spiritual strength.

This is unnecessary. God can deal with our anger. Some of our most positive role models in the Bible felt and expressed anger toward God, and it made their relationship with him stronger.

**Uncontrolled emotions**

A sudden death introduces some level of trauma into our lives, and this can unleash a flurry of emotion—or none at all. Shock creates a sensation of numbness—emotionally as well as physically—so it's not unusual to shut down your feelings in a traumatic situation. You might be wondering why you're not crying. Shouldn't you be crying? If you really loved this person, you would be crying, right? Well, not necessarily. Sometimes shock freezes our emotions. That is fairly normal.

> **When it is dark enough, you can see stars.**
>
> **—Ralph Waldo Emerson**

But emotions have a way of squeezing out. We can only clamp them down for so long, until they come rushing out somewhere else (though sometimes in alternate forms, like angry outbursts or self-destructive behavior). So you might get through the funeral without tears and then cry for three days straight.

And it's not just sorrow. Emotions of fear and guilt and anger and worry and self-doubt and silly joy can run rampant, seemingly on their own. When you've experienced a sudden loss, you've sustained a major blow to your emotional equilibrium. All your settings are out of whack. Don't be surprised what comes out.

Sometimes our fears and doubts about the goodness of life are overshadowed by what is happening to us and around us. The death of a loved one is one of these times. But we are told to have faith, to look beyond the surface of things, and to allow the possibility that miracles exist. Grief shuts us down emotionally for a while, but if we keep a part of us open and receptive to life, we may find the blessing after all.

*My Creator, blessed is your presence. For you and you alone give me power to walk through dark valleys into the light again. You and you alone give me hope when there seems no end to my suffering. You and you alone give me peace when the noise of my life overwhelms me. I ask that you give this same power, hope, and peace to all who know discouragement, that they too may be emboldened and renewed by your everlasting love. Amen.*

Love is a gift we give. Love is a gift we receive from others. Even those who are gone continue to give and receive love. Love knows no fences, no restraints, and no confinements.

# Denial Helps . . . for Awhile

Psychologists used to talk about five "stages of grief." That terminology is less in vogue these days, but it's still a helpful way to understand our processes. The first of these stages is *denial.* This happens in any experience of loss, but it tends to be especially strong in cases of sudden grief, dealing with the shock of a loss we didn't expect.

You don't want to admit it at first. You want to pretend that everything is the same as it always was. When you lose someone you love, you know they're gone, but you still expect them to walk through the door at any moment.

Even when your mind has grasped the reality of this loss, your instincts are still lagging behind. You find yourself setting a place at the table for them or planning what you'll give them for Christmas. Especially in the first month or two, there are many heartbreaking moments as you remind yourself again and again of your loss.

When someone has had a limb amputated, they often still feel phantom pains or itchiness in the missing part. It's a trick of the nervous system. The neural pathways are so deeply ingrained that it's hard to shut them down. Apologies for that stark word-picture, but losing a cherished loved one is much the same thing. That person has become a part of you. Your life has interacted with their life so intensely that you still feel as if they're just in the next room.

**The pain of losing someone dear to us can be overwhelming. We feel bereft and alone, confused and lost, certain that we will hurt like this forever. But with God's strength, we can move on.**

Denial is normal, a protective measure God has wired within us. When real life gets too painful, we ignore it for a while. You might be tempted to scold yourself for this, but don't. You might be tempted to wonder: "What's wrong with me? Am I going crazy? Am I losing touch with reality?"

Relax. It's part of a regular process of dealing with a bad situation. God has allowed our minds to ease into these harsh circumstances. Denial is a temporary gift designed for our protection.

How long should you experience denial? That varies. Some losses are harder to take than others. Let's just say it's generally a matter of months rather than years. There are stories of parents who have been so devastated by the loss of a child that for years afterward they refused to change anything in the child's room. That's not healthy. At a certain point—months rather than years—you need to accept your loss and move forward in your life.

There is a natural process of recovery, and it usually starts with denial. But you don't need to follow any sort of schedule. Most people experience denial as long as they need to. When it's not helpful anymore, they naturally move on. Yet, occasionally, people get stuck in denial. They might need a helpful nudge from a pastor or counselor.

So don't rush yourself through this. Don't panic if you keep dreaming about your lost loved one, or even if you hold conversations with them. This can all be very therapeutic, actually. Denial is part of the healing process.

Don't let others rush you through this, either. "It's been three months already! Why can't you face up to reality?" That might sound good on a soap opera, but it's a really stupid comment. It often takes six or eight months, even more, for denial to do its healing work. And reality? You want to talk about reality? The reality is that you have lost someone very close to you, someone who inhabited your heart, someone who will *always* have a home in your heart. You just have to rearrange the furniture in there, and that may take some time.

# What You Can Do

***Get counseling.*** Long ago, only crazy people went to psychologists, then it was all the rage, and now it's just . . . expensive. And why would you need professional help when you have a book like this, right? The truth is that you have experienced a major loss, a sudden loss, and that will affect you in major ways. It would help to have an expert to track the specific details of your recovery. Not forever, just over the next year or so. And it need not be a psychologist; a pastor might serve as a good first consultation.

***Get practical help.*** We've discussed the practical details that often frustrate the recovery process. You might need a trusted friend or relative (but someone who is not as shaken by the recent loss) to take care of some of these matters for you—the funeral and burial in the short term, the will and insurance in the midterm, cleaning the house and going through files in the long-term. People may offer to help with some things, and that's great, but you might need to ask someone to manage these matters in your stead. Trust is a major factor.

***Take your time.*** You don't need to get all healed by next Thursday. God has created a process by which it takes a year or two to get over these things, and some issues can last even longer. You can try to rush the process, but that will probably mean you'll have to come back later and redo part of it. People around you want you to feel better, so they'll urge you to put on a happy face. For your own long-range health, resist all attempts to rush you. God will restore you in his time, at his pace.

***Talk with the one you've lost.*** This happens naturally for some, but others fear it's a sign of madness. In the case of sudden loss, it's extremely important for you to get the "uns" out of you—the unfinished business, the unanswered questions, the unresolved anger, and the uncontrolled emotions. And if you believe in life after death, in the grace of God your loved one might actually be able to hear you. So tell them how much you loved them. Yell at them for not being more careful. Urge them, even now, to open up to the embrace of God. Ask for their forgiveness if there were issues between you.

***Talk honestly with God.*** Even if you have to say, "I'm mad at you right now because you took someone I loved," keep those lines of communication open. God took that kind of talk from Moses, David, Job, and Jeremiah—he can take it from you.

***Share with others who are grieving.*** Don't be afraid to talk about the one you've lost in the weeks and months afterward—especially with others who were close to the one who passed. But let these conversations be full of grace. Understand that the others are experiencing a range of emotions just as you are. If everyone starts crying, that's fine. If people start accusing each other, defuse it with love and understanding. Don't try to "fix" anyone else's grief—just as you wouldn't want to be "fixed." With others you can experience comfort and release.

***Take steps to rebuild your life.*** This won't happen all at once, of course, but you can begin to make choices, when you're ready, to live again. Reject the notion that it's not fair for you to live well when your loved one is gone. Survivor's guilt is common, and it often senselessly keeps people from moving forward. What kind of life would your loved one want you to have? Sometimes people are afraid to move forward because they fear losing the memory of the one they've lost. Create memorials. Find ways to hold that dear one in your heart forever. But don't let grief sabotage your future life.

*God will never leave thee,*
*All thy wants He knows,*
*Feels the pains that grieve thee,*
*Sees thy cares and woes.*
*Raise thine eyes to heaven*
*When thy spirits quail,*
*When, by tempests driven,*
*Heart and courage fail.*
*When in grief we languish,*
*He will dry the tear,*
*Who His children's anguish*
*Soothes with succour near.*
*All our woe and sadness,*
*In this world below,*
*Balance not the gladness,*
*We in heaven shall know.*

—General Hymn #286, *Book of Common Prayer*

Teach us to know, God, that it is exactly at the point of our deepest despair that you are closest. For at those times we can finally admit we have wandered in the dark, without a clue. Yet you have been there with us all along. Thank you for your abiding presence.

Dear Lord,
In my hour of grief, be the guiding light that directs me through my pain. In my day of despair, be the gentle hand that leads me out of the dark woods. In my moment of need, be the tower I lean upon for strength and assurance. In the night of my anguish, be the presence that comforts and soothes me like a mother to a child. In the time of my suffering, dear Lord, be my friend and constant companion. For this I am grateful. Amen.

*Chapter 3*

# Times of Deep Sorrow

***It's just sad to lose someone you love, and many people report a sapping, soaking sorrow at their very core. They wonder if they'll ever be able to enjoy anything ever again.***

The Lord is near to the broken-hearted, and saves the crushed in spirit. Many are the afflictions of the righteous, but the Lord rescues them from them all.

—Psalm 34:18–19

# Missing His Aunt

Daniel was just 11 when his aunt died. Aunt Maysie was like a second mother to him, often caring for Daniel and his little brother when his mom had to work. His aunt didn't have much money, but she liked to buy them gifts. These were often little impulse purchases she'd pick up at a checkout counter, but the boys treasured them. It showed she was thinking of them. Daniel remembers a little Pez dispenser she got for him once. It was a silly little thing, but he loved it, mostly because it came from her.

But Aunt Maysie outdid herself for his eleventh birthday, when she saved up enough to buy him a Game Boy. She thought it might be a lot of fun and keep him out of trouble. She was right. It was his best gift ever.

Then she got sick suddenly, and it was worse than anyone expected. In a short time, Maysie died, and Daniel's parents broke the news to him. He remembers that moment vividly, though it happened more than a decade ago. There was suddenly a heavy feeling. He couldn't breathe. He knew his mom and little brother were crying, but he couldn't cry, not at that moment. He didn't really know what to do.

So he ran to his room.

There in his bedroom, alone, the tears finally came. He felt a deep sorrow for many months afterward, finding it hard to concentrate on his schoolwork. Sometimes he would play his Game Boy for hours, trying to shut out the pain. But it kept coming back. He knew his beloved aunt was gone forever, and no one could ever replace her.

Daniel learned that the sorrow fades over time. For him, the pain dissipated throughout the next year, but it never went away completely. Sometimes now, a decade later, he remembers Aunt Maysie and misses her. There's a shadow of that deep sorrow still in his heart. But he also smiles gratefully, remembering all the great things she did for him.

*Lord, let my sorrows become seeds, watered by my tears. Let the dirt and, well, manure of my environment provide nutrients for my growth. Let each downward turn of my experience be a root thrust into the nourishing soil. Let the scorching sun and slicing rain become my lush green leaves. Let the bracing winds teach this seedling to stand strong. Let me branch out through the seasons and bear fruit in time.*

*In the dark sea of my despair, dear God, I am afraid, lost, and alone. But I will not give up hope. I will cast out my heart one more time into the deep waters and await your loving salvation. Amen.*

Where before my heart was like a desert, desolate and empty because of my deep despair, God has set the rain of his loving grace upon me and I am beginning to bloom again. Where before my soul was a wasteland, with no life because of my suffering over this terrible loss, God has tilled new ground and set the foundation for a mighty fortress of healing to rise upon once-spoiled lands. I am a garden overflowing with new, lush life, and I owe it all to the grace and love of God.

*We linger at the grave, O God, needing you to lead us through this valley of fading bouquets and crushing grief into the land of the living. When it's time, go with us to buy flowers for our tables along with flowers for the graves we visit.*

# Trying to Avoid Your Loss

If you have lost someone you love deeply, you will go through a time of deep sorrow. The intensity of the grief may vary, as well as the ways we show it. The time of deep sorrow might be long or short. But it will happen. Of course we try to avoid it at first. We attempt various tactics to keep from confronting the full force of our loss. We focus on our work or our faith. We valiantly adopt a positive mental outlook. We throw ourselves into activities of various sorts. These are walls we put up to protect us from sorrow. The classic "stages of grief," first popularized by Elisabeth Kübler-Ross, have helped us identify some of these walls.

*Denial* seldom actually rejects the reality of the loss. Though there might be daydreams and wistful moments when we temporarily forget that the person has passed, usually denial just downplays the severity of the loss. We try to go on with our lives just as we did before. We fight back the tears. We keep a stiff upper lip. We remind ourselves that everything will be all right.

**When I thought, "My foot is slipping," your steadfast love, O Lord, held me up. When the cares of my heart are many, your consolations cheer my soul.**

**— Psalm 94:18–19**

Sometimes our religious faith plays into this denial. Make no mistake: Faith is a helpful, healing force. But sometimes we use it to shield us from necessary emotions. "God is good all the time. I know my loved one is in heaven, so why should I be sad? All things work together for good." There's nothing untrue about those statements, but if they make you feel guilty for crying, they're counterproductive.

*Anger* is defined as the next stage of grief, though they don't always go in order. Anger is an emotional response, but it moves outward, not inward. It can serve as another deflection from our deep sorrow. It is a step forward from denial, because we're admitting we've suffered a loss that has hurt. We want to lash out at those who have hurt us. (We'll discuss anger more thoroughly in a later chapter.)

The next stage, *bargaining,* is hard to explain, because it encompasses a wide range of behavior. In a way, it's a step back toward denial, because it seeks a quick remedy to the pain you're beginning to feel. Some people make vows to God at this point: *If you get me through this, I will become*

*a missionary.* Some who have lost their mates suddenly get remarried, expecting that the joy of their new union will ease their sorrow. (Sometimes that works, but usually it puts extra strain on the new relationship.)

This is also the time when various addictions come to the surface. If you've ever struggled with drugs or alcohol, you will be tempted to salve your pain with those substances. People also throw themselves into gambling, shopping, eating, exercising, or even video games. These are all attempts at quick fixes. So don't be surprised when these temptations emerge. Be ready for them. The truth is, these quick fixes won't solve anything. At best, they're distractions. At worst, they're destructive. (You might even want to have a friend on call, someone who can hold you accountable and keep you from doing something you'll regret later.)

Note that these stages aren't necessarily bad for us. They're part of the process. Denial is sort of an emotional numbness, protecting us while we deal with the new reality. Even anger and bargaining, while they may lead to hurtful behavior, aren't always bad. Be careful about bad choices here, but don't rush through these steps. You'll be in these stages as long as you need to be. There's no schedule you need to follow. If you think you're stuck in a particular stage, get a professional opinion, but generally we need to accomplish certain things in each stage, and once we do, we move on.

So let these stages do their work. Denial protects us for a time. Anger reactivates our hearts. Bargaining gets us going again and teaches us (the hard way) that there's no easy way out.

*Why are you cast down, O my soul,*
*and why are you disquieted within me?*
*Hope in God; for I shall again praise him,*
*my help and my God.*

—Psalm 42:11

*All the words that I gather,*
*And all the words that I write,*
*Must spread out their wings untiring,*
*And never rest in flight,*
*Till they come where your sad, sad heart is,*
*And sing to you in the night,*
*Beyond where the waters are moving,*
*Storm darkened or starry bright.*

—William Butler Yeats

When the anguish of loss overwhelms us,
and we feel there's no reason to live.
We must look deep within to find meaning
and to know we've still so much to give.

# Into the Pit

The only way out of the pain is through it. Keep moving through the process. Unfortunately, the next stage is the pits—specifically, the pit of depression. When you finally realize there's nothing you can do, the full reality of your loss comes crashing down on you. The sadness hits. You get weepy. You get lethargic. You can't taste your food. You don't care about the things you used to enjoy. You don't sleep well. You go through your days in a haze.

This is when the people around you start trying to cheer you up—and you just want them to go away. It's been six months since the funeral. Isn't it time you got over it? Frankly, they don't know what they're talking about. You need to spend time in the pits. It's the way you heal.

If you were to break an arm, the doctors would put it in a cast, immobilizing it so the bone could heal properly. It's the same thing when your heart gets broken with grief. Your emotions will naturally go into depression—immobilizing them—so they can heal properly. It takes time. If you rush it, you'll probably sink back into depression later. You will be frustrated by it. You will want the depression to be over and done with. One day it will be, but for now you're languishing in the pit of deep sorrow.

This sorrow affects people differently. It's very common for people to respond as 11-year-old Daniel did, by going off by himself to process his feelings. Many struggle with two conflicting needs—the need to be alone with their grief and the need to get support from others. In some cases they withdraw from social commitments and later wish they hadn't.

In the opening pages of *A Grief Observed*, C. S. Lewis candidly described his experience of grief over the loss of his wife. He made mention of this double-mindedness regarding society—wanting to be with people, but not really wanting to interact with them: "If only they would talk to one another and not to me."

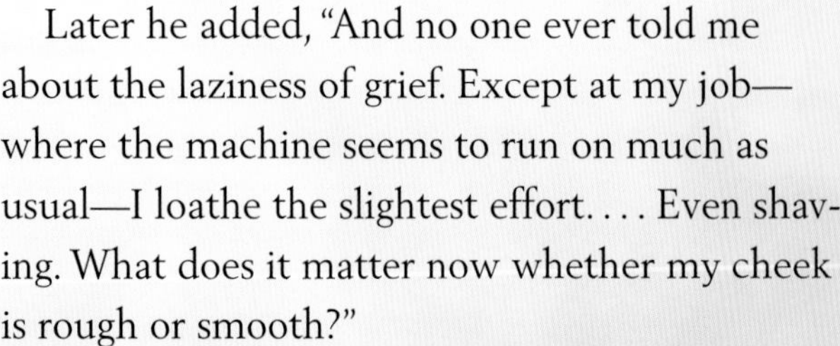

Later he added, "And no one ever told me about the laziness of grief. Except at my job—where the machine seems to run on much as usual—I loathe the slightest effort. . . . Even shaving. What does it matter now whether my cheek is rough or smooth?"

*What does it matter?* That could be the banner for our time of deep sorrow. It's easy to stay in bed all day. Do you really have anything to get up for? This sorrow is a kind of death, actually. After trying all those avoidance techniques, we finally do the only thing we *can* do—nothing.

Sad to say, some people take this literally. Some take their own lives or let themselves waste away. Doctors report that some people actually get the symptoms of the diseases and injuries that killed their loved ones. A daughter dies of brain trauma in an accident, and the father gets headaches. A husband dies of a heart attack, and the wife feels chest pain. Some ancient cultures would place a living wife on the funeral pyre of a dead man. That's a cruel image to think of, but that's sort of the same thing many modern widows and widowers do to

themselves. *What is there to live for? Let me die with you.*

As with the other stages, there is work to be done here. The depth of our sorrow testifies to the depth of our love. By grieving, we honor the one we've lost. By joining them in the death-*like* experience of depression, we make an important final connection with them. This is an important task. It must not be cheated. As painful as it may be, the deep sorrow has to happen.

But enough is enough.

Have you ever been part of a crowd giving some luminary a standing ovation? It can go on and on, until finally the honoree waves the crowd down. "Enough! Enough!" Some modern worship leaders will sometimes direct a congregation: "Let's give a round of applause to God!" And of course it's a standing ovation. He is the Creator of the universe, after all. But how long does *this* last? How can you stop clapping for God? Eventually people realize that they have important stuff to move on to, and the ovation dies down. Besides, they'll have all eternity to applaud God.

**May God's love make your grief bearable.**

Here's the parallel. Sometimes people get stuck in deep sorrow because they feel the lost loved one deserves more grief. "How can I even think of being happy when I loved him so much?" But at some point, the ovation is enough. You will have honored the memory of your love enough, and it will be time to move on to other important stuff. At a certain point, the dearly departed himself would say to you, "Enough! Enough! Thank you. Now get on with your life."

There's a wise tradition in the Jewish faith. One year after someone dies, their tombstone is unveiled in a ceremony that marks the end of an official mourning period. Of course this doesn't mean that all sadness is over, but it's a helpful way to turn a page in your life, to focus on living rather than dying.

As psychology experts have studied the recovery process over the last half-century—denial, anger, quick fixes, and depression—they have found that it usually takes about a year. There are exceptions to this, naturally, and certain factors that might extend or shorten the process, but you can expect a year or so of emotional downtime. It's God's way of "restoring our soul."

*Give sorrow words.*
*The grief that does not speak*
*Whispers the o'er-fraught heart*
*and bids it break.*

—Shakespeare, *Macbeth*, IV, iii

*Dear Lord,*

*My prayer is simple today. I grieve, and I hurt. Give me the strength to feel all this pain. I sometimes feel that I can't survive it, but I know that with your love and help, I can. Thank you for your abiding love. Amen.*

What a friend we have in Jesus,
All our sins and griefs to bear!
What a privilege to carry
Everything to God in prayer!
O what peace we often forfeit,
O what needless pain we bear,
All because we do not carry
Everything to God in prayer!

—Joseph M. Scriven, "What a Friend We Have in Jesus"

*Dear Lord,*

*I'm in a swamp of sorrow and feeling unrelenting darkness of grief. Please send your angels to shine their light on the beauty of your creation so I can have a few moments of joy today. Tomorrow may be easier, but I really do need as many angels as you can spare today. Amen.*

*I know, God, that this too shall pass. Even as I am in the midst of this pain and despair, I can see the light at the end of the long, dark tunnel. I can see the light of your love for me and the wisdom these trials will give me. I can see the brighter day ahead filled with laughter. Knowing this, I carry on toward the light.*

# Coping with Deep Sorrow

Any quick tips or industry secrets that would make your sorrow easier—well, they would be counterproductive, wouldn't they? You *need* to go through this time, and it's tough. These suggestions are not ways to lessen the pain but ways to make sure that you're grieving efficiently, that you're not making this process any longer than it has to be, and that you're taking care of yourself in the meantime.

***Find a caretaker.*** You need someone who will be a combination nursemaid and drill sergeant, not a cheerleader who will try to make you feel better. It's someone who understands the grieving process, who will make sure you're eating right, sleeping as well as you can, avoiding addictions, and attending to your important duties. Take some care in finding your caretaker and communicate the "job description" clearly. This might be a family member, but it shouldn't be someone who is feeling the loss just as deeply as you are. You are very needy right now, and maybe you'll repay the favor in future years, but right now you need to be on the receiving end.

***Don't feel bad about feeling bad.*** People will try to cheer you up. Accept their good wishes, but don't let them lay a guilt trip on you. If you are in this time of deep sorrow, you have no business smelling roses, picking daisies, or looking on the bright side of life. You need to feel bad; that's your job right now.

***Talk about your sorrow.*** You will find a few people you can share your feelings with. These might be family members or friends who share in the loss. It always helps to talk. People always want to say the right thing to help you, so you might need to tell them, "You don't have to say anything. Just listen for a while, and let me know you understand."

***Draw near to God.*** You might have a love-hate relationship with God right now. That's to be expected. You're angry with him. You need him more than ever. Don't let your anger drive you away from this supreme source of support. Talk to God each day, even if just to say, "I don't want to talk to you today." One of the often-overlooked truths of scripture is this: *God mourns too.*

***Begin thinking about ways you might honor your departed loved one a year from now.*** Give yourself a future. And remind yourself that you honor this person not only with agony but with action. "Dying" with them (that is, experiencing this deathlike grief) is one way to show the depth of your love, but living life in their memory is good too. On your good days, you might begin brainstorming ways to do that.

*My grief feels as if it will never subside, God. Everything within me melts like wax when I wake up in the morning and realize all over again what has happened. My life is forever changed. Sometimes I wonder if you are there, but I know you have promised always to be with me. Please hold me close. Amen.*

*Help me grieve and go on… go on in new ways you will reveal to me, Lord, as I make my faltering way as far as I can. Hold me while I name and mourn all I have lost, weeping and wailing like the abandoned child I feel I am. Then, in time and with you to lean on, I can focus on what I have left.*

*Chapter 4*

# Times of Guilt and Regret

***The things you wish you had said. Were there issues left unresolved? How do you get past the guilt?***

As far as the east is from the west, so far he removes our transgressions from us. As a father has compassion for his children, so the Lord has compassion for those who fear him. For he knows how we were made; he remembers that we are dust.

—Psalm 103:12–14

# A Son's Death

The 2010 movie *Rabbit Hole* stunningly depicts a couple's difficulty in dealing with the loss of their young son. As the movie begins, we sense that something's wrong. Becca (played by Nicole Kidman) is making excuses, avoiding social engagements, withdrawing. We slowly learn that there has been a loss in the family. Husband Howie (Aaron Eckhart) wants to move forward, to get on with the healing, but Becca is resisting. As we put the pieces together, we realize that their 11-year-old boy was fatally struck by a car when he chased the family dog into the street.

There are supportive friends and family around them, but Becca and Howie don't always want to be comforted. Becca is particularly put off by a support group Howie has dragged her to. After someone in the circle has uttered the platitude "God needed another angel," Becca says, "Why didn't he just make one? I mean, he's God, after all. Why didn't he just make another angel?"

As the film progresses, we get glimpses of this couple individually and together, coping with their loss. They bicker. They stop talking. We learn they haven't been intimate since the accident, eight months ago.

Howie stays up at night watching a video of their son at play. Becca, who has been throwing out the child's pictures and giving away his clothing, "accidentally" erases the video. The two of them have trouble getting their healing in sync. There are some desperate attempts to break out of the rut of grief. A new job, an affair, selling the house—none of which really work. They blame each other, and the dog, for their tragic loss.

Then Becca hunts down the teenage driver of the car that killed their son. Not for revenge, just to talk. And their conversation is a masterpiece of subtle healing.

"I just really wish I'd driven down a different block that day," the teenager says. It was an

accident, everyone agrees, but in a second meeting the teenager confesses something that's been gnawing at him. He might have been going 31 or 32 mph, not the posted limit of 30, he's not sure. "I'm sorry," he says.

"Okay," says Becca.

At one point Becca has a heart-to-heart with her mom, who also lost a son, Becca's brother, 11 years earlier. She asks about the pain of loss. "Does it ever go away?"

"No, I don't think it does. It changes though."

"How?" Becca wonders.

"I don't know. The weight of it, I guess. At some point it becomes bearable. It turns into something you can crawl out from under and carry around like a brick in your pocket. And you even forget it for a while, but then you reach in for whatever reason, and there it is . . . which can be awful, but not all the time. It's kind of—not that you like it, exactly, but it's what you've got instead of your son. So you carry it around. And it doesn't go away."

*They shall all know me, from the least of them to the greatest, says the Lord; for I will forgive their iniquity, and remember their sin no more.*

—Jeremiah 31:34

Time and space cannot separate those who love. For love transcends all limitations, rises above all boundaries. Love knows only the realm of the unlimited.

# Guilt Complicates Grief

Guilt and regret often haunt those who have lost a loved one, making the pain more complicated. Sometimes the guilty feelings are pressed down deep, where they can't be talked out or reasoned away. Sometimes family members blame each other, or think they're being blamed, and thus the grief poisons relationships.

Will the sorrow ever go away? Not entirely. There will always be an empty place in your life. But by facing up to the guilt and regret, by putting these emotions in their place, you can avoid getting tangled up in blame and shame. You can keep the healing process from being harder than it has to be.

***Guilt about the death.*** Especially in the case of a sudden death, people sometimes blame themselves, at least partially. Whether or not it's logical, they can begin to spin the story so that they're responsible.

- "He was coming to pick me up when he had that accident. If I had made other plans, he'd still be alive."
- "She caught that flu from me, I'm sure. And with her immune system, she couldn't fight it. I should have been more careful."
- "We never should have let her go on that hiking trip. We should have seen the danger."
- "I should have told him to go see a doctor. Well, I did, but if I'd been more insistent, maybe they would have caught the disease in time to save him."

**It is not just the storm cloud that brings us the opportunity for growth and understanding, but the hopeful expectancy of the rainbow behind it.**

Guilt feelings are especially prevalent in the case of suicide. Though the person was ultimately the sole cause of his or her own death, the act leaves everyone else wondering what they did wrong.

***Guilt about the ease of the final days.*** In cases where someone lingers for a time before death, some survivors feel bad about things they said or did—or did *not* say or do—in those final days. After all, this is the final opportunity to get everything squared away, to offer apologies, to erase misunderstandings, to share secrets. Sometimes these conversations go badly. Sometimes they don't happen at all. Any less-than-perfect outcome can leave people feeling guilty.

Often loved ones carry regrets about not being at the bedside when someone passed on. Some

would have to travel from a distance, and most have their own schedules, so it's hard to ensure one's presence at the final moment. Still, this is a common concern: "If I were a better friend/son/daughter/brother/sister, I would have made it a priority to be there."

***Regrets that the relationship was not better.*** People are flawed, and relationships are hard. As a result, there are always things to regret about any relationship. You can always find something you wish you had done or hadn't done. A death creates a kind of "highlight reel" of a relationship. Our emotions toy with our memories, and we tend to focus on the best and worst behavior of ourselves and the other person. Regrets surface, now that it's too late to do anything.

It doesn't help that everyone else remarks on how great the deceased person was, or that friends and family sometimes take this occasion to compare themselves to each other. (*Who was the most loyal child? Who was the most trusted friend?*) All this can chafe against an already guilty conscience.

***Survivor's guilt.*** Psychologists have noted a phenomenon from accidents, disasters, and war in which some people are killed and others survive. The survivors have a hard time accepting not only that others died, but that they themselves lived. *A mistake was made,* they feel. *I don't deserve life any more than they did, but now they're gone and I'm not.*

This can result in various problematic actions, some of which may be subconsciously motivated. Self-destructive behavior can be an attempt to set right the "mistake" God made, and so a survivor might take high risks or give in to addictions. Listlessness might be seen, since life makes no sense anymore, so why bother to live it? Low self-esteem might be demonstrated in conversation and personal choices.

On occasion, "survivor's guilt" can motivate a person to act responsibly, even courageously, in order to make their life mean something. They might see themselves living life in place of the one who died. This has its dangers, since it puts enormous pressure on ordinary life, but it can yield positive results.

*Bear with one another and, if anyone has a complaint against another, forgive each other; just as the Lord has forgiven you, so you also must forgive. Above all, clothe yourselves with love, which binds everything together in perfect harmony. And let the peace of Christ rule in your hearts.*

—Colossians 3:13–15

*Sweet hour of prayer, sweet hour of prayer,*
*that calls me from a world of care,*
*and bids me at my Father's throne make all*
*my wants and wishes known.*
*In seasons of distress and grief my soul*
*has often found relief,*
*and oft escaped the tempter's snare by your*
*return, sweet hour of prayer.*

—William W. Walford, "Sweet Hour of Prayer"

# The Problem with Guilt

At this point you're probably expecting to read something like this: *Don't be silly. You don't need to feel any guilt or neglect. You did all you could do. There's no reason to feel bad about what you did or didn't do. You're blameless. So, focus on the positive and get on with your life.*

The problem is, that's not necessarily true.

You might actually have good reason to feel guilt and regret. You probably haven't acted perfectly in your dealings with the one you've lost, either in their final days or in the rest of life. Chances are there were things left unsaid, undone. When you think of those things, you feel bad.

But let's sort this out.

It's important to distinguish between ***guilty feelings*** and actually ***being guilty.*** Some people have extremely sensitive consciences. They say,

"I'm sorry," at the drop of a hat, anyone's hat. They feel guilty for anything and everything, even if they had nothing to do with it. Maybe you're one of these people.

Others seem to have no conscience at all. They breeze through life without recognizing how they might be hurting those around them. They might actually *be* guilty of all sorts of misdeeds, but they never *feel* guilty. Let's hope you're not one of these.

It is one of life's great ironies that the people with the greatest guilt feelings are usually those with the least actual guilt, and vice versa.

So figure out which of these you are—or, more precisely, where you'd belong on this continuum. How sensitive are you to guilt feelings? Way too much? A little too much? An accurate amount? A bit too little? (And if you never feel guilt at all, you're probably not reading this chapter.) You might want to ask some friends to confirm your analysis.

With this in mind, you can begin to evaluate those regrets and guilt feelings you have. If you are generally a person who is oversensitive to guilt feelings, then you know that most of the blame you're putting on yourself is misplaced—maybe not all, but most.

For instance, Mary might feel guilty because she asked Bill to pick her up after work and he died in a car accident on the way. She blames herself for his death. But does this make sense?

As Mary thinks about her own tendencies, she realizes that she often feels guilty about things. (She felt personally responsible for the mortgage crisis because she made a late payment.) So then she tries to consider the reality of it. What really caused the accident? A reckless driver (not Bill). Was it unusual for her to ask Bill for a ride? Not at all. And if he weren't picking her up that night, he might have been running other errands and running the same risk.

Guilt feelings do not necessarily indicate any actual guilt. These feelings merely indicate your sensitivity.

As you continue to sort through your feelings of guilt and regret, it's also important to consider ***reasonable expectations.*** In Mary's case, it was perfectly reasonable to ask Bill to pick her up.

But what if there were other factors involved? What if she knew Bill had just gotten home from working for three days straight and was very sleepy? What if he was a new driver who had never been out on the road alone? What if he was unfamiliar with the stick shift in the car he had to drive? And in spite of all these things, Mary just insisted that he come get her. If that's the case, then things are more serious for Mary. Her actions were not reasonable, and she may actually bear some of the guilt for Bill's accident.

**Confession without lament is not honest; our grief is evidence of trust in God.**

Reasonable expectations are often a problem for family members when a loved one is terminally ill. They want to be at the bedside, sure. But when it goes on for days or weeks, they need to make tough decisions. They have jobs. They have other members of the family to care for. They might be visiting from out of town and need to get back home. Meanwhile, the dying one might be making greater and greater demands. What's reasonable and what's not?

*In my trials, Lord, walk with me;*
*in my trials, Lord, walk with me;*
*when my heart is almost breaking, Lord,*
*I want Jesus to walk with me.*
*When I'm in trouble, Lord walk with me;*
*when I'm in trouble, Lord, walk with me;*
*when my head is bowed in sorrow, Lord,*
*I want Jesus to walk with me.*

—African American spiritual,
"I Want Jesus to Walk with Me"

*Turn to me and be gracious to me,*
*for I am lonely and afflicted.*
*Relieve the troubles of my heart,*
*and bring me out of my distress.*
*Consider my affliction and my trouble,*
*and forgive all my sins.*

—Psalm 25:16–18

***Lord in Heaven, work a miracle in our hardened hearts and shine the light of your love upon our gloomy corners, where we now cower in our fear and pain. Bring us this day our daily bread, our daily hope, and our daily strength, and then bring it to us again tomorrow. Lord, with your help we can overcome any difficulty, rise above any challenge, face any fear, and cope with any loss. Shower us with your healing love like manna for the hungry in heart and soul.***

Man of Sorrows, see my grieving heart this day. Keep me from feelings of shame, though, as I let the loss wash over me. For this is a part of my life too, the life only you could give me: to learn what it means to let go.

# Regrets in a Relationship

Chad had had a tough decision to make. His dad was dying, but no one knew how long he had—days, weeks, maybe a month. Meanwhile there was a one-week vacation trip Chad had planned and paid for—it would be costly to cancel. And with his demanding job, it was the only week he'd be able to get away for a long time to come. He was ready to stay by the bedside, but his brother said, "No, go ahead. I'll man the fort here. Take the trip. I'll let you know if anything happens."

As it happened, his father died five days into the trip. Chad grabbed a quick flight back, earlier than planned, but he wasn't there for his father's final moments. He has some regrets about that, but fortunately he has the support of his brother, who maintains that it was perfectly reasonable to go on the trip.

As we deal with regrets about our relationship with the deceased, we need to remember that no one's perfect—not us, not the deceased. Any loving bond has some hurt in it. Of course there are things we regret about how we have treated others. And despite the saintliness we often attribute to the recently departed, we need to admit that they have mistreated us too. You might be tempted to shine the spotlight of your memory on every moment in which you acted badly toward the one you've lost. Don't do it. Every relationship has its down times. According to reasonable expectations, were you a decent son or daughter, brother or sister, husband or wife, parent or friend? Not perfect, but decent?

**We know that all things work together for good for those who love God.**
**—Romans 8:28**

As we continue the sorting process, we come to a fork in the road. The paths lead to either ***shame*** or ***forgiveness.*** The truth is that sometimes our guilt feelings really do indicate that we're guilty. Sometimes we have failed to meet reasonable expectations. We might have to admit that we're really *not* a decent son or daughter, brother or sister, husband or wife, parent or friend. So... what can we do about it?

Well, you have several options. One is to keep blaming yourself. Hold this sense of guilt within you for the rest of your life. Let it damage future relationships. Let it sabotage your relationship with God. Let it prevent you from finding true satisfaction in life.

That's not such a good option.

Another option is to shrug off the guilt and regret. Pretend that it's no problem. Hey, you did what you could, no big deal. As far as the morality of the whole human race is concerned, you're still ahead of the curve. This isn't such a good option either, because guilt is tenacious. It gnaws at you. And like the kid in the movie who has heard everybody say, "It was an accident; don't worry about it," you still can't sleep because maybe you were going 32 in a 30 mph zone.

Your best option is, of course, to find forgiveness. And that can get tricky.

*My loving Lord,*

*My guilt is heavy upon me. And I'm afraid I can't make things right. I feel terrible about those I've hurt, people I've disappointed, and trouble I've caused for those I love. There is so much I wish I could undo.*

*As you know, it's complicated. We all have "issues," and I can easily turn those issues into excuses, but I'm going to stop running away from this. I've done wrong, and I need your forgiveness. Please restore my relationship with you, and help me to make peace with everyone I've hurt, including myself.*

*I rely completely on your grace. Amen.*

# Forgiveness

This is a good time to recommend that you ***seek professional help*** if you need it. But choose your professional help wisely. Some psychologists don't get the spiritual side of forgiveness. Some pastors don't get the psychological side. And everyone has a really hard time understanding grace.

One of the good things about this time of guilt and regret—as difficult as it might be—is that it gives you a better sense of who you are. Are you a good person who occasionally does bad things; or a bad person who occasionally does good things; or a weak person who can't always do what's expected of you; or an imperfect person just trying to get along in a twisted world? That might be worth thinking about.

Then here's the thing that a lot of people don't get about forgiveness: Seeking it is an admission of guilt. In casual parlance, we say, "I beg your pardon," and the response is often, "It's nothing." But if we're truly seeking forgiveness for something, it can't be dismissed so easily. It's not "nothing"; it's definitely something. So if you have sorted through your guilt feelings and discarded the things that are merely concoctions of your overactive conscience—but you still worry about things that you might have done wrong in relation to the loved one you've lost—you need to confess. But to whom?

Chances are, the person you feel you've wronged is the one who has passed away. How can you get forgiveness now? You might long to hear him or her respond, "I understand. I forgive you. I still love you." And of course that can't happen now. Does that make forgiveness unattainable? Not necessarily.

If you believe in the afterlife, if you believe that your loved one is living on in some form, if you believe that he or she is now with God—then why can't you ask them for forgiveness? Even some counselors who don't believe in the afterlife recommend carrying on conversations with a loved one after death, just to get out all those emotions. How much more appropriate should that be for those who trust in a God who cares about both you and your loved one?

So go ahead, if you need to say you're sorry, say it. Say it directly to the one you've lost. Maybe you'd feel more comfortable including God in that conversation. "God, I don't know if my mom can hear me and forgive me, but I know you can. Please make things right."

Two other possibilities here: Many people make their confessions to a priest or pastor. Even if that's not part of your normal routine, it might be a good way to break free of the power of guilt. You might also want to sit down with family members and talk honestly about the things you feel bad about. Do this only if you're pretty sure your confession won't ignite a firestorm of misunderstanding. (There might be other family issues you might come clean about.)

Sometimes clergy assign ***acts of penance*** for people who confess sins. These are often misunderstood. The penance doesn't *earn* forgiveness, which is a free gift of God's grace; it's a *sign* of the sincerity of one's heart in seeking forgiveness. Along the same lines, if you feel you need forgiveness, you might come up with some action that makes this desire concrete. Volunteer for a ministry or charity. Make a donation in the loved one's name. Do good deeds for other family members. Not that these actions will bring about forgiveness, but they might prove to you that you're serious about what you're saying.

It's one thing to seek forgiveness. It's another to *change your life.* This time of guilt and regret is a tough one to go through. But if it forces you to evaluate your behavior and make improvements, then you can leave this time a better person than you were when you entered.

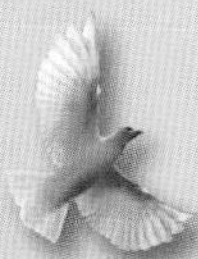

Our journey together does not end when one person dies. We continue to walk the same path, only now one of us walks on solid ground and the other floats alongside in the realm of pure spirit.

*Chapter 5*

# Times of Loneliness

***The sense of solitude can be palpable. There is a hole in your heart in the shape of the person you've lost. How will you ever fill it?***

It is the Lord your God
who goes with you; he will not leave
you or forsake you.

—Deuteronomy 31:6

# Missing Mom

Amanda used to talk with her mom every day, at least once a day, sometimes more. Though she was 40, with her own apartment, her own business, her own social life, she still checked in. She had plenty of friends, but her mother was probably the best. Maybe that came from being the only daughter in a family of sons. She and her mother shared a special bond.

Then her mother got sick. Cancer. She fought it aggressively for several months, but the cancer spread. Amanda had to tell her mother the prognosis: two weeks to live.

A woman of great faith, Amanda's mother used her final weeks to prepare everybody for her death. She planned out her funeral service in detail, as a celebration of her life rather than a sobfest over the loss. The funeral was both. There were plenty of tears, but there was also great laughter, as friends and family recalled their special moments with her. This woman was already enjoying the bliss of heaven.

Yeah, but Amanda was still on earth, missing her best friend terribly.

"The phone doesn't ring anymore," she says. "I used to count on that, once or twice a day." She works at home, by herself, so there are long, lonely days. She would go out at night, chatting with friends at dinner, but even that was no cure for the deep loneliness she felt. Amanda did what she could to help her dad cope with the loss of his soul mate, but he was wounded by this tragedy too. There wasn't much he could do to help her.

In the midst of all this, there was a romantic breakup. A guy she had been seeing for some time, well, it didn't work out. Amanda's already tender emotions were thrashed once again. She was in a bad way. Steeped in loneliness, she found it hard to summon the energy to go out, which made her even lonelier.

It's still a struggle for her, a year and a half later, but she has taken some steps to climb out of this pit. For one thing, she got a little more involved with the church she had been sporadically attending. Amanda even went on a mission trip, where she didn't have to talk much—she could just work. She forged important relationships there. Later, she even reached out to help one of those friends through a crisis. There has been a slow move outward, out of the cubicle of loneliness that has held her.

But she's still lonely. And she misses her mom.

*Blessed be the God and Father of our Lord Jesus Christ, the Father of mercies and the God of all consolation, who consoles us in all our affliction, so that we may be able to console those who are in any affliction with the consolation with which we ourselves are consoled by God.*

—2 Corinthians 1:3–4

***Time helps, Lord, but it never quite blunts the loneliness that loss brings. Guide and bless my faltering steps down a new road. Prop me up when I think I can't go it alone. Most of all, Kind Healer, thank you for the gifts of memory and dreams. The one comforts, the other beckons, both halves of a healing whole.***

# Private and Public Grief

You're not alone. There are other relatives and friends who have been hurt by the loss of this loved one also. Many of them are going through the same process you are. That's why we have funerals—to bring together the grieving community, to share our sorrow.

And there is a wider community around you, a group of believers who want to help you through the crisis. They're not always sure what to say or do, but they're concerned about you. They want to encourage you, empower you, and salve your wounds.

Ironically, grief can be a very private thing. Many people prefer to withdraw from the crowds when they're hurting. They feel emotionally out of control, and they don't want to embarrass themselves in front of others. Some feel a need to put on a strong face, to seem "together" in this crisis, so that people whisper that they're "taking things remarkably well." But at a certain point, they just wish everybody would go away so they can sort through their feelings on their own.

Maybe that's your story; maybe not. There are some people who prefer to grieve in the company of caring friends. But for the most part, mourning is an activity that's both private and public.

So then why do we get so lonely?

**When the Lord calls our loved ones home, he leaves a gift of memories in exchange.**

***You have lost an irreplaceable person.*** This goes without saying, but we shouldn't ignore it. Amanda lost her mom, who was essentially her best friend. No one else is going to call her every day. In cases where one spouse has lost another, the survivor can be utterly bereft. That's their soul mate, the one they had woven themselves around for years and years. How is life lived without them?

And that question is not just *How can I summon the energy to go on?* It is, quite literally, *How*

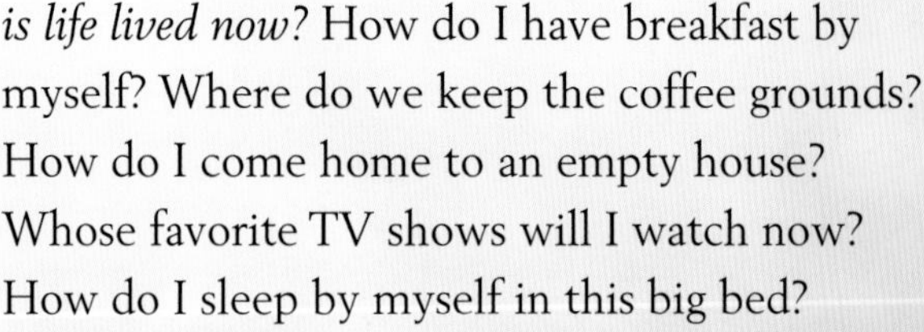

*is life lived now?* How do I have breakfast by myself? Where do we keep the coffee grounds? How do I come home to an empty house? Whose favorite TV shows will I watch now? How do I sleep by myself in this big bed?

Details of this loss keep surprising you. Wives report that they miss all the irritating things their husbands used to do. They would give anything to pick up dirty socks, to put the cap back on the toothpaste. A widower goes on a business trip and sits on his hotel bed: Who do I call to say I got here safely? Who else cares?

Loneliness can be expected when you lose a person you have shared your life with—a parent, a child, a sibling, or a spouse. That person cannot be replaced. Some widows and widowers remarry quickly, hoping to fill that gap, but this often turns out badly. The new spouse cannot replace the old—he or she must be an entirely new element in one's life. And it's true that new elements—whether a new spouse or just new friends or experiences—will eventually ooze in to fill the empty space in your heart. But this will take time.

***People don't get it.*** They try to help, but they usually don't succeed. As a result, the grieving person feels even more alienated. It's like being in a foreign land where no one knows your language. They're talking, but their words don't mean anything to you. You're trying to express the pain in your heart, but it doesn't register with them.

People often describe the grieving process as "surreal." Why? Because their reality has fundamentally changed, but no one else's has. It's like a sci-fi movie where one person is in a different dimension, walking among people who are unaware. A grieving person wants to stop the world and say, "Don't you get it? Life can't go on as usual when I have suffered this terrible loss! How dare you go about your business when my world has collapsed!"

This makes the loneliness of grief especially resistant to all attempts to cure it. Even if the mourner gathers up the oomph to get out and socialize, he or she is still lonely in a crowd, because no one is speaking the right language. No one gets it.

***They avoid you, you avoid them.*** Funerals are important events, where a grieving community gathers to honor the dead, but even more so to support one another. But what happens after the funeral, a week or a month or six months later?

Leslie used to go to church every week, showing up bright and early and chatting with friends long after the closing hymn. Now she comes late and leaves early. Why? Her husband passed away not long ago. To her credit, she knows she needs to connect with God and the community of faith, but she can't deal with the people right now. They'll want to know how she is, and she'll say she's fine, and they'll say, "Really?" And she'll say what they want to hear. The thing is, they feel awkward and she feels awkward. No one knows what to say, but they have to say something to show they care—but do they really want Leslie to pour out her guts about how her faith has been challenged and her heart has been broken and her life has been ruined but other than that she's just peachy? It's easier to just avoid them.

And they avoid her too. This is common. In casual connections, people just don't know what to say. In formal invitations, it's just easier to invite someone else. It's not usually an intentional blacklisting, but as people fill out their social calendars, they think twice about inviting someone who's grieving. It might be uncomfortable, they think. It might be too soon. This is especially true when someone has lost a spouse. Other couples in their social circle may not know how to deal with a newly single person. They might be afraid that it will awaken everyone's grief to see this widow or widower alone in a room full of couples.

This avoidance is not evil, just really short-sighted. Awkwardness is not the worst thing in the world. Sometimes it's the price you pay for love. Meanwhile, avoidance is a common short-term strategy, adding to an already crippling loneliness.

**The circle of life remains unbroken by the experience of death. Like a wheel forever turning, the sun continues to rise and set, the tides continue to swell and withdraw from the shore, and those who have died continue to move along the wheel, even though our eyes cannot discern them.**

***Your relationship with God may be shaky.*** Don't get this wrong: A little shaking up might be the best thing for your faith. We see this often in scripture. When people question the things they thought they had figured out about God, it opens them up to a whole new experience of him. But it's kind of scary when it happens.

So if you've been questioning things about God, beliefs you've held tightly for many years, it might not be a bad thing. But it does sort of pull the rug out from under you. And if you're used to turning to God as your ultimate cure for loneliness, you might be less apt to do this in your present grief. He is still there for you, but given what happened, you might find it harder to trust in his care.

*Lord, save me from my comforters. I know they mean well, but sometimes they say the silliest things. If one more person tells me to "cheer up," I think I'll slug them. (Lord, give me patience!) It's hard enough careening through every emotion you created without having these "friends" directing traffic.*

*All right, Lord. I know I need to receive their gifts of love and be grateful, but it's hard sometimes. Help me to have patience. Amen.*

# What Can You Do?

People come for a funeral, sometimes from far away, to share your grief. You need to spend time with them. It's a time of high energy, high emotion, a whirlwind of activity, with all sorts of people, some you hardly know, rushing around to help you. You're probably kind of glad when it's over.

But then there's a funnel effect. You get a few cards and flowers in the following week, and then . . . not much. That's when loneliness really kicks in. The distractions are done. You're withdrawing, and your friends are avoiding you. Is there anything you can do to assuage your loneliness effectively, or do you just need to wait it out?

Yes and yes. You *need* a time of loneliness to process your loss and begin to heal, but you can also take steps to keep the loneliness in check.

***When people "comfort" you, listen to their hearts (not their words).*** People may say some stupid things. Their words may be sappy or silly or inappropriate or mildly offensive, but they're just trying to help. Think about the times in the past when you've been in their shoes, searching for something to say to comfort someone. It's not easy. We send pastors to seminary to learn stuff like that. The rest of us mutter reassurances like, "It's all for the best"; "He's probably happier now"; or "You'll forget all about her."

The words really aren't important, are they? They're rather irrelevant. If you videotaped these encounters and turned off the sound, you'd get the essential elements: the loving look, the supportive hand. These people want to say the right thing; they just don't know what that is. Don't hold that against them. Receive the warm wishes of their heart, no matter what the words.

***Find a friend who gets it.*** This is probably someone who has lost someone, preferably one who has had time to work through the grief. This needs to be someone you can be honest with.

They need to sense when you want to talk and when you don't. They mustn't try to "fix" you. They just need to be there for you.

***Set boundaries as needed.*** If you find a friend like that, you will probably begin leaning on that person in the same ways you leaned on the person you lost. You might begin to overstep reasonable boundaries. Talk about this. Together, you and your friend can set some guidelines for reasonable interactions. (How many calls per day is too many? How many visits per week? Etc.)

***Let the tears flow.*** Some people will do anything to avoid crying in public. It's not "manly." It makes your makeup run. It seems childish. The dearly departed wouldn't have wanted that. People have all sorts of reasons, but none of them hold water, so to speak. This is your time to grieve. You're allowed to cry. You're supposed to cry. People expect it. So open the floodgates of your heart, and let your emotion flow. No need to run to the restroom to sob in private. Just have plenty of tissues available.

Tears are a cleansing agent. This is true physically as well as emotionally. God has wired us to cry in times of distress, and this qualifies. It's healthy to weep and unhealthy to hold back. If it makes people uncomfortable, that's their problem, not yours.

**Our loss touches God's heart deeply. He created the one for whom we grieve, and he knows very well the irreplaceable nature of the relationship we shared. God does not minimize or misunderstand our pain. He weeps with us and longs to console us with his love.**

***Watch out for the rebound.*** In your time of loneliness, you'll be tempted to grab at shallow relationships that promise fulfillment but don't deliver. Be very careful here. Recognize your vulnerability right now. Go slow in any new relationship, romantic or platonic. (We might expect rebound relationships when someone has lost a spouse, but it also happens when parents lose a child. One parent might seek comfort in an affair because the other spouse is also grieving and unable to provide comfort.)

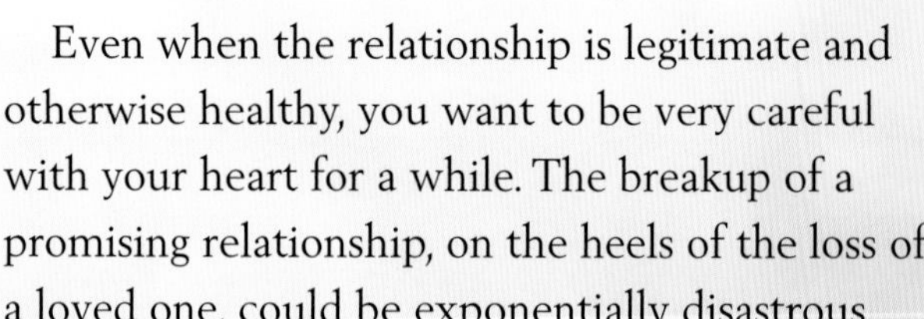

Even when the relationship is legitimate and otherwise healthy, you want to be very careful with your heart for a while. The breakup of a promising relationship, on the heels of the loss of a loved one, could be exponentially disastrous.

***Find a group that accepts you.*** You can help yourself by assembling a small corps of caring friends. Look around for the people who seem especially interested in helping, those who say, "Let me know if there's anything I can do," and who really mean it. Take them up on that offer. Ask them to check up on you throughout the next year or two. If they're truly gifted in caring, they'll understand, and they'll appreciate the request. Look also for people who have gone through similar losses. (If you can't identify such comforters yourself, you might ask your pastor to suggest some people from the congregation.)

***Train them to help you.*** As mentioned earlier, people with caring hearts don't always say the right thing. They don't always do the right thing either. You may need to tell them how to care for you. What do you need? This starts with the funeral arrangements and proceeds through the grieving process. You can't expect people to read your mind. Ask them to sing a song, help with your taxes, babysit your kids, or call you every Friday. You might feel selfish about that, but you're actually just helping the process work. The task is to provide comfort for you. You need to be the foreperson of your crew, telling people how to accomplish this. In most cases, they will be grateful for the direction. Assure them that they don't always have to have something to say. Often it's best just to be there. And sometimes you don't want to talk about your grief; you'd much rather hear about a ball game or a movie.

***Treasure your private times.*** Psychologists talk about introverts and extroverts. This distinction has little to do with how much of a show-off you are; it's about where you get your energy. Introverts gain energy when they're alone and expend it in public. After being with people for too long, they need to go off by themselves and recharge. Extroverts draw energy from others and find it taxing to be alone. You may find this applicable to your grieving process. If you're an extrovert, you may need a group of caring friends who can work through your grief with you. If you're an introvert, you will need many private moments along the way to refuel.

Maybe you've had too many private times lately. But you will be moving out into the world more as your loneliness dissipates. Even then, you can value your time alone, seeing it not as a time of rejection but as a time of personal growth.

As you emerge, *look for others to comfort*. It might seem like a distant hope at this point, but you will emerge from the grieving process with renewed spirits and restored health. And you will have gained something important—empathy for others who have suffered loss. You will have learned about comforting from the vantage point of the one who receives comfort. That's a valuable piece of education that will equip you to provide effective comfort to others.

So pay attention as you continue on the road to health. Take notes. Someday you can use your pain for the gain of others.

*Lord, dismiss us with thy blessing,*
*Hope, and comfort from above;*
*Let us each, thy peace possessing,*
*Triumph in redeeming love.*

—Robert Hawker, "Benediction"

*Through companionship, gracious God, that you send to travel alongside me, I feel myself warmed, uplifted by friends, family and those who've traveled the same road.*

—Miguel de Unammo

*Let Love clasp Grief lest both be drown'd . . .*

—Alfred, Lord Tennyson, "In Memoriam"

*Lord, please help me remember that though I have suffered a great loss, the love I shared with my dear one remains. The body may be buried, but the person can remain a joyful presence in my life. It's hard to remember that in my darkest hours, Lord. Please hold those joyful memories for me until I can hold them myself. Thank you, Lord, for your steadfast presence.*

In the silence of despair, we hear nothing but the lonely beating of our own heart. In the silence of faith, however, rhythms of the world around us remind us that God's heart beats nearby.

***While I wait for this piercing pain of loneliness to pass, Great Comforter, cradle me as the wailing, lost child I've become. I feel your warming presence and know that no matter how lost I feel right now, you hold the most important truth and are whispering it now: "You are my beloved child. I am with you."***

When we lose a spouse, we must take time to go within and reaffirm our connection with God. Once we are able to feel God's presence in our lives, we will know that we already have all we need to move beyond the grief and begin to live and love again. Sometimes I want to be alone. But thank God you're there, my friend. Sometimes I need a good cry.

Chapter 6

# Times of Anger

***You might feel anger—toward people around you, toward yourself, toward God, perhaps even toward the loved one who died. You are hurting, and it's natural to lash out—but how can you avoid doing damage?***

Be angry but do not sin; do not let the sun go down on your anger.

—Ephesians 4:26

# Anger and Grief

Sam punched a hole in the wall. With his fist. In the hospital.

Well, it was the hospice unit, where his mother had just died. He was full of emotion, and he didn't know what to do with it. This wonderful woman who had given him life and taught him to live—it wasn't fair that she would die. He needed to lash out, to attack, to express his rage. So he hit a wall.

The nurses went ballistic. They weren't used to such displays of violence. Perhaps they were afraid of what Sam would do next. They rushed to call the on-site counselor, who ambled to the scene.

Sam was sitting in a chair, staring into space, rubbing his knuckles.

"So," said the wise counselor, drawing up the seat beside him. "How's your hand?"

"Not bad. Sorry about the hole in the wall."

"Oh, that." The counselor looked up to inspect the damage. "That's a nice one."

"I kind of lost control."

"It happens."

"I can pay for it."

"I'm not worried about the wall," the counselor continued in his easy tone. "We'll get a maintenance crew up here, they'll patch it up like new. They love that stuff. I'm more concerned about you."

"Yeah, I shouldn't get upset like that, huh?"

"No, that's not what I'm saying. You *should* get upset. I'd be hopping mad myself. I'm just wondering, how did you know there wasn't a stud there?"

Sam was surprised at this reaction. "Um, I didn't."

"That's the thing, see? Punching a hole in drywall, you maybe bruise your hand a little. But you hit a two-by-four like that, and we're taking you to the ER. That's the last thing you and your family need right now, right?"

"Yeah."

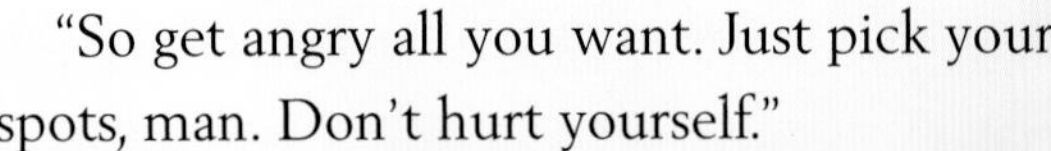

"So get angry all you want. Just pick your spots, man. Don't hurt yourself."

That's a crucial lesson in anger management. Anger will happen, but you can always choose what to do with it. As you deal with your loss, you may enter times of anger, and with good reason. There's nothing wrong with being angry—just be careful not to damage anything important. Especially yourself.

> **For as the heavens are higher than the earth, so are my ways higher than your ways and my thoughts than your thoughts.**
>
> **—Isaiah 55:9**

The Bible verse we've used to introduce this chapter is worded in an interesting way. "Be angry but do not sin" (Ephesians 4:26). Other translations say "In your anger, do not sin." Either way, it assumes that you will get angry, but it gives you the responsibility to control your actions.

The same hospice counselor had another case with a family that was bickering from day one. Four daughters and three sons came to visit their mother in the hospice facility at various times

in the final days of her life. When their visits overlapped, there was trouble. The counselor was called in more than once to defuse heated arguments between the siblings so the mother could rest peacefully. He finally convinced the family to honor their mother by trying to get along with each other. Their petty fights weren't helping anyone—especially her.

That reasoning seemed to work . . . until the mother died. All seven of her children were in the room for her final breaths, and then all hell broke loose. The counselor got a call from the staff. "You'd better get down here. They're throwing chairs."

That's an example of inappropriate behavior. These people had every right to be angry about their mother's illness and death, and some of that anger might spill over toward other family members. But it was clear that this family chose anger as their basic emotional response. They were in their element when they were picking fights. And they seemed to have little sense of appropriate limits.

Anger happens, but we choose our behavior.

*How long, O Lord? Will you forget me forever? How long will you hide your face from me? How long must I bear pain in my soul, and have sorrow in my heart all day long?*

—Psalm 13:1–2

*Lord, I'm upset and angry at you. You have taken away someone I loved. How could you do this? "God is love," I have read in the Bible since I was a child. Is that true, or just a slogan? Because you don't seem very loving right now. I'm just being honest here, and I've always been taught that if I have a complaint to take it to the source. You're the source.*

*I'm not perfect, I know that. But that's not the issue here. I'm not saying I deserve to live a pain-free life, but you have done something really awful here, or you let it happen, which seems like the same thing. I want some understanding. I want some peace. I know: You're God and I'm not, and I'm trying to hang in there with you, but it's tough. So help me out, please!*

# Mad About You

The experts who identified the "stages of grief" saw that anger was the second stage, following denial. While the stages don't always go in order, there is a progression. Once you get past denial, you get the full experience of your loss, and it hurts. Anger is a natural response to pain. "I don't deserve to hurt like this. I want to get back at whoever is responsible."

Some people get stuck here, becoming angry and bitter. Others try to rush through it. But, just like denial, anger has a job to do. It's an important step in a God-given process.

Many of us have trouble with anger in general. We all feel it, but we differ broadly in how we express it. Some are volcanoes, spewing out angry feelings and then moving on as if nothing happened. Others are slow cookers, stewing in hurt feelings for days or weeks before letting anything out. Many religious folks feel guilty when they get angry, so they hide it. But the feelings are there, and they will find a way to come out, in healthful or unhealthful ways.

When you finally face the reality that you've lost someone close to you, it's natural to feel angry. But at whom? For what? It's not always clear. That's what makes this anger so tough to deal with.

Have you ever had a bad day when you were ready to lash out at anyone and everyone for the slightest problem? You were a bundle of anger looking for a reason to exist. That's sort of like the anger involved in the grieving process. You may not be sure what you're angry about, but you know something is wrong and you're upset. You feel a pain that you don't deserve. Someone ought to pay for that! And so you might let your anger out in a scattershot manner, holding grudges for silly things, taking offense at any raised eyebrow, and barking at everyone around you. Or you might focus it all on one poor soul who doesn't really deserve it. Then again, you might turn it on yourself.

You might be angry with yourself for not seeking the best medical care for the departed. You might scold yourself for things you said—or left unsaid. You might be mad at yourself for not spending more time with your loved one.

You might be angry at friends and relatives for not helping out enough with the funeral or other arrangements or for not being there in those dying days. You might be angry with the staff at the hospital or the nursing home or the funeral home.

You might even be angry with the person you lost. This can be especially difficult. You feel it, but you don't want to admit it. It seems wrong to dishonor their memory with such complaints, but this feeling festers within you. They never got around to buying life insurance. They left you out of the will. Or maybe their death was largely their own fault, through smoking or drinking or not seeing a doctor. If only the person wasn't so stubborn, he or she would still be here today!

Ultimately, many people feel angry with God. This is often the hardest to admit. We believe in a loving God who wants what's best for us, right? Then how could he allow us to feel so much pain? This is especially true if your loved one has been taken in the prime of life. It seems wrong, and God should be held responsible for that. Shouldn't he? When feeling this type of anger, many people begin living double lives, spiritually. They act as if they're on great terms with God, but they're secretly holding a serious grudge. As a result, they find it hard to pray like they used to.

# Just Cause

At some level, anger is a yearning for justice. We feel we don't deserve pain, so we respond angrily when we feel it. The simplest case is a schoolyard fight where some bully hits you for no good reason. You want to achieve justice by causing him the same amount of pain he caused you. Not that anyone actually analyzes it like that on the playground, but from our earliest years anger is grounded in a desire for fair play.

Because of this, we often make certain allowances. Imagine that you are elbowed, hard, as you walk down a busy street. Your anger kicks in, and you want to yell, "Hey, pal, watch where you're going!" But then you notice that the culprit is a guy struggling down the street on crutches. You immediately make allowance for the fact that it was his difficulty, not his recklessness, that gave you a poke in the ribs.

We are constantly playing judge and jury as we go through life, showing our anger to those who deserve it and excusing others. And we don't just get angry at our own mistreatment. The same anger can rise up within us when we see injustice against others—whether it's in a news report about a foreign country or an example of prejudice in our own society.

Or perhaps the death of someone we love.

When a loved one dies, there are several "justice issues" that might fuel our anger. Yes, we are feeling personal pain that we feel we don't deserve, but we might also be upset that our loved one was denied the opportunity to live longer. This seems especially unfair when the person is young or even middle-aged. We expect people to live "threescore and ten," or nowadays even longer, so it seems unfair for someone to be taken sooner. If they were in pain when they died, that gives us even more reason to be angry. They certainly didn't deserve that.

Of course, if they've been the victim of negligence or violence, we burn in our rage toward the culprits, but often we're left with no one to

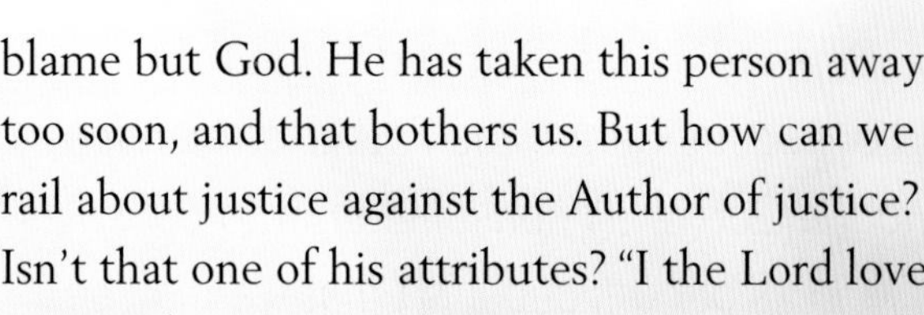

blame but God. He has taken this person away too soon, and that bothers us. But how can we rail about justice against the Author of justice? Isn't that one of his attributes? "I the Lord love justice," he says (Isaiah 61:8).

This leaves us with a major disconnect. We are angry, no question about it. It seems apparent that our loved one was unjustly taken from us, and we are hurting as a result. But if God is ultimately responsible, what can we do with that anger?

*Comfort me in my day of need with a love that is infinite and true. Ignore my lack of desire to forgive and forget. Fill my anger with the waters of peace and serenity that I may come to accept this situation and move on to a greater level of understanding and knowing.*

# Passive Aggression

Many people of faith become passive aggressive. This sounds like a contradiction, but it's a very common approach, especially among religious folks. Passivity comes from a desire not to show anger. For those who've been taught that anger is wrong, this is a learned response. These people *feel* anger—that's the aggressive part—but they hold it back, refusing to act on it—that's the passive part. And that might sound like a good way to function in society until you realize that anger usually doesn't go away unless it's expressed. It's like steam in a pot. You can cover the pot, but eventually the steam will build up and blow the lid off. Passive aggressive people try to hold back their anger, but it comes out in all sorts of oblique ways. The mantra of the passive aggressive person: "I don't get mad; I get even."

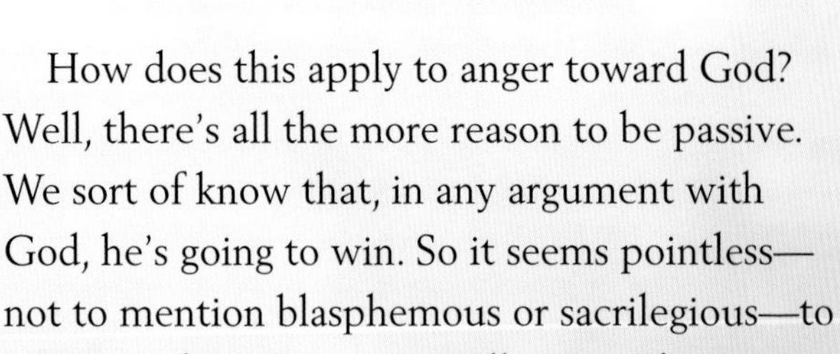

How does this apply to anger toward God? Well, there's all the more reason to be passive. We sort of know that, in any argument with God, he's going to win. So it seems pointless—not to mention blasphemous or sacrilegious—to scream at him. But we're still angry. The steam is building up. Where can it go?

One guy arrives late to church each week. His friends think he just likes to sleep in, but that's not the issue. He's mad at God for various problems in his life, and this is one little way of getting back at the Almighty. (This does not mean that everyone who's late to church has issues with passive aggression.)

Some lead double lives. On the surface they're upstanding Christians, but they secretly harbor doubts or misdeeds that they don't want to confess. "I'll worship you, God," they seem to be saying, "but you can't have all of me."

Some take their anger out on themselves, engaging in self-destructive behavior. For many, the quashing of their angry impulses does its own damage, causing stress, hypertension, even heart problems.

In Eugene O'Neill's great play *A Moon for the Misbegotten,* a grizzled old farmer complains to his daughter about the son he hates. "When I think your poor mother was killed bringing that crummy calf to life! I've never set foot in a church since, and never will." This is a very common sentiment. Thousands of people refuse to go to church because they blame God for someone's death. But there are also thousands of people *within* the church who hold similar grudges against their Creator. Even though these churchgoers go through the motions of faith, their grudges are holding them back from true intimacy with God.

We ask over and over again, "Why?" But the answer does not come readily. Only with time and healing can we begin to understand and to know that a grand design is at work in our lives, and that the Grand Designer has not abandoned us or forsaken us at all.

# Honest Anger

What can you do with your anger? First, *accept it*. Don't feel guilty about it. It's just another part of the recovery process. Like denial, it's an important but temporary step toward healing.

***Be honest in your anger.*** Think about a couple's first date. They dress nicer than they normally dress; they act nicer than they normally act; they show more interest than they normally show—all in the hopes of finding someone who will love them as they really are. That relationship might start as a surface attraction, but if it's going to grow, they'll both need to develop more honesty.

When someone passes away, the community of family and friends usually honors their memory by focusing on the good things rather than the bad. But you need to get past that surface level if you're going to develop a lasting relationship with the memory of this loved one. You have to get honest. It might seem disrespectful to scold this person after they've passed, but it could be your way of saying what needs to be said. In a way you're saying, "I want to treasure your memory as the person you really were, not some phony, airbrushed image."

The same thing might be said about God. You might feel funny about scolding God, but there's a rich biblical tradition of people who did just that. Moses was great at it. David wrote the book of Psalms partly for that purpose. If you want to get past the first-date stage with God, you have to be honest. Tell him how you really feel—and then listen for how he feels. If there's anger involved, that's not a problem. God can take it.

***Talk about your anger.*** But take care in choosing the person you talk to. You might need to tell them up front that you're not looking for an argument, you just need someone to listen. This is especially true if you're expressing anger toward God. Most people will feel a need to stand up for God, but that's not what you need right now. You need to vent. Perhaps, as you talk it through, you and your confidant will come to some new understandings about God and the events of your life, but that's not necessary. At this point, you just need to let out some steam.

***Be careful about fallout.*** The problem with anger is that it can do damage. If you lash out in anger against everyone who crosses your path, you'll hurt a lot of feelings, destroy some relationships, and maybe even cause injury. So look for harmless ways to unfurl your angry energy. One woman bought a set of old dishes at a yard sale and took them out to the woods. Then she hurled those dishes at the trees, smashing them to bits, while hollering at everyone with whom she was angry.

***Use your angry energy to accomplish something.*** One man used his angry energy to tackle some cleaning projects he'd been avoiding for years. Another guy was so upset about losing his wife that he renovated his basement in record time. It was something he had always promised her he would do but had never gotten around to. One good thing about anger is its energy. If you can redirect it toward building up instead of tearing down, that's a good thing. One classic case is the Mothers Against Drunk Driving organization, founded by a grieving mom to do something positive in society. But don't set your sights too high, too early. You don't need another disappointment right now. Yet you do need a positive place to put your energy. So. . . get some exercise, volunteer in the neighborhood, or help a friend move (but only if the friend *wants* to move). When anger makes you want to be active, be active. Just be careful about punching walls.

*I know that at times I will be troubled, I know that at times I will be belabored, I know that at times I will be disquieted, but I believe that I will not be overcome.*

—Julian of Norwich

*Chapter 7*

# Times of Fear and Worry

***Bereavement often unleashes a collection of worries about yourself and your own future. How will you go on?***

Though I walk through the darkest valley, I fear no evil; for you are with me.

—Psalm 23:4

# Practical Matters and Grief

Doris was living the dream: a hardworking husband, two great daughters in high school and college, and a great house in the suburbs with a pool. Early on, it was decided that she would stay home with the kids while her husband earned a living. Money was tight at times, but they made that work. When the girls were older, Doris picked up various part-time jobs, but she never got established in a career.

Then her husband died of a heart attack at the age of 58. Doris was devastated. She had lost her life-companion. True, they had gone through some rough patches in their marriage, but he had always been a loyal husband and father. She worried about how her daughters would cope with the loss.

In the weeks following the funeral, Doris found even more to worry about. She had never paid much attention to the family's finances. That had always been his department. But now it fell on her. And as she put together the

pieces, a picture fell into place. Her husband had struggled to afford a comfortable home for her and the kids, but there was never much left over. There was some equity built up but many years left on the mortgage. There was no life insurance. There wasn't much of a pension to tap into. The savings account was slim.

Now, on top of her grief, Doris had a whole new set of worries. Could they keep the house? Could she pay college tuition for her two daughters? Where could she find a full-time job that would pay anything close to what she needed?

The following years were hard. Doris landed a full-time secretarial job. The house was eventually sold, its equity used for a down payment on a modest condo. In time, both daughters graduated from less-expensive state schools, their way paid through loans, scholarships, their own wages, and the last of their family's savings.

It worked out for this family, but not without worries, fears, and sleepless nights. A number of worries crop up for those who have lost loved ones. Some are, as with Doris, practical in nature. Others are emotional or deeply personal.

*Though we stumble, we shall not*
*fall headlong, for the Lord holds*
*us by the hand.*

—Psalm 37:24

*Under his wings I am safely abiding, though*
*the night deepens and tempests are wild;*
*still I can trust him, I know he will keep me,*
*he has redeemed me and I am his child.*
*Under his wings, what a refuge in sorrow!*
*How the heart yearningly turns to his rest!*
*Often when earth has no balm for my healing,*
*there I find comfort and there I am blest.*
*Under his wings, O what precious enjoyment!*
*There will I hide till life's trials are o'er;*
*sheltered, protected, no evil can harm me,*
*resting in Jesus I'm safe evermore.*

—William O. Cushing, "Under His Wings"

# Worries About Practical Needs

It seems a little inappropriate when you're dealing with issues of life and death to focus on money. Yet that's exactly what most of us must do. A death changes the lives of those connected to the departed one. Especially within families, we're not just connected, we're *intertwined*. The loss of one person within a family system can raise a number of very down-to-earth issues.

***Finances.*** When it's a wage-earner who has passed away, there is of course a major effect on the family's finances. When it's the primary wage-earner, as in Doris's case, the effect can be devastating. Often there are insurance policies and other payments that will ease the blow, but there's still a major shift in the way things work.

In many cases, a surviving person is stuck dealing with a confusing array of investments, policies, and accounts. If they haven't been involved in the family finances before, it's a challenge to make the right decisions now. In addition, there are various hucksters offering various schemes for your family fortune. How will you make the right decisions?

**Every tomorrow has two handles. We can take hold of it with the handle of anxiety or the handle of faith.**

**—Henry Ward Beecher**

***Living Arrangements.*** When one person in a home passes on, it changes the structure of that home. In Doris's case, the bleak financial situation necessitated a move. In other cases, it might be decided that a widow or widower really shouldn't live alone. If a young child has lost a sole parent, there are important questions about where the child will now live. These decisions can cause worries for everyone involved, both for those opening their homes to others (and wondering if they have enough room) and for those who don't want to be a burden on others.

***Division of Labor.*** When people live together, they get used to certain patterns. A home operates a certain way as all its members do various tasks. One cooks the meals; another makes the coffee. One drives; another navigates. One balances the checkbook; another does the shopping. One sends birthday cards to relatives; another squashes bugs with a shoe. This division of labor is most obvious with a married couple, but it can be seen in any home, with two people or ten. And when one person passes away, that means certain jobs will have to be taken on by others or go undone. This can cause all sorts of worries. *Who will cook the food? I don't know how! Who will pay the bills? I can't add! Who will drive the car? I haven't driven in years!*

One important division of labor concerns child care. When a parent of young children passes, it might create a crisis that's not about finances but about children. Who's watching the kids when the surviving parent earns a living?

***The Future.*** Many people fret about the future even without a death involved, but the passing of a loved one can add fuel to that fire. Our closest family and friends populate our hopes and dreams. We have pictures in our minds of ourselves enjoying retirement with a spouse, being walked down the aisle by a father, teaching our child to ride a bike, and so on. Obviously, along with the emotional pain we suffer at the death of a loved one, there's also a shake-up of those dreams. We have to envision a new future without them, and that can be scary.

*Give us grace and strength to forbear and to persevere. Give us courage and gaiety and the quiet mind... give us the strength to encounter that which is to come, that we may be brave in peril, constant in tribulation, temperate in wrath, and in all changes of fortune, and, down to the gates of death, loyal and loving to one another.*

—Robert Louis Stevenson

# Fears for Others

Naturally, when we've sustained a loss, we tend to turn inward. We deal with our own pain, doubts, and fears. But as we begin to heal, our attention turns outward, and it lands first on those around us who have suffered losses as we have. It can be a beautiful thing to show love and concern for others, but it can also add to the weight of worry on our hearts.

***We worry about the children.*** Children are resilient, but they're also impressionable. They tend to recover rather well from the loss of a family member, but there are often additional circumstances that trouble them.

Lynn was 12 when her older sister passed away. It was cancer. The whole family was shocked and saddened, of course. As the only other girl in the family, Lynn was perhaps more affected by the death. What made it far worse for her was her father's reaction. Grieving his older daughter's death, he distanced himself from the younger one. He very consciously refused to get close to Lynn because he feared he would lose her too—and he told her so. This did damage to her emotionally, as you might expect.

As a grown woman still sorting through the resulting issues, Lynn now says simply, "Make sure the kids are okay." Whenever there are children in the immediate or extended family of the departed one, they need to be communicated with; they need to be loved.

**So do not worry about tomorrow, for tomorrow will bring worries of its own. Today's trouble is enough for today.**

**—Matthew 6:34**

So, some level of concern for children is appropriate, but remember their resilience. They go through a similar recovery process to that of adults, sometimes in a shorter time frame. You don't need a master's degree to figure out the perfect thing to say—just be honest and caring. Hear their questions. Ease their concerns. One danger is that a high level of worry in *you*

might instigate worries in *them*. So don't hover, nag, or browbeat. Hug, talk, and listen.

***We worry about those closest to the deceased.*** "How is Dad dealing with Mom's passing? He's been focused on meeting her needs for years. Does he have any purpose in life, going forward?" These are legitimate concerns, and it helps to have people around the immediate family who are asking these questions. Attention must be paid, and a reasonable level of concern will motivate us to check in on Dad, to make sure he's okay.

But of course worry can grow to an unhealthy point. We can manufacture all sorts of worst-case scenarios and let those fears affect us. We might see some ordinary manifestation of grief and blow it out of proportion. "Dad broke down and cried today. I think he's losing it." Well, no, he's not losing it. Crying is a fine thing to do when you've lost your mate.

One danger here is that Dad would recognize the worry in his kids and thus keep from expressing his true emotions, so no one will worry about him. That would not be healthy for him. So, in your times of fear and worry, use your basic level of concern to show wise care to those who might need it, but don't overreact to the normal processes of grief.

***We worry about our own mortality.*** We go through life trying not to think about death. When someone we love passes away, we get a grim reminder. If we have lost a spouse, who is near in age to ourselves, we recognize that we're getting older ourselves. If we have lost a parent, we take one step up the generational tree—perhaps we are now the patriarch or matriarch. If we have lost someone younger, we see again how fragile life can be. There are no guarantees. We could go at any moment.

Christian faith is a cure for the fear of death. (This is true of some other religions as well, but not all.) We "may not grieve as others do who have no hope," the apostle Paul wrote (1 Thessalonians 4:13). Indeed Christianity is about hope—the hope of a relationship with God that blesses us now and unfolds in even greater blessing hereafter. "Dying is gain," according to Paul (Philippians 1:21). A better life awaits.

And yet it's natural to fear death. No matter how great our faith, the afterlife is unknown territory. It's like the first day of school for a six-year-old. No matter how great you say it will be, it's still quite terrifying. In our times of fear and worry, we might latch onto this basic fear and let it govern our thoughts for a while. And then we worry about worrying—surely this is a sign that we've lost our faith.

Relax. Unplug the fear of death with prayer and common sense. As Jesus asked, "Can any of you by worrying add a single hour to your span of life?" (Matthew 6:27). On the contrary: Experts tell us that worry can actually subtract hours from our life span. Worrying will not help you approach death without fear. Prayer will.

*Lord Jesus,*
*Your are medicine to me when I am sick,*
*Strength to me when I need help,*
*Life itself when I fear death,*
*The way when I long for heaven,*
*The light when all is dark,*
*And food when I need nourishment.*
*Glory be to you forever.*
*Amen.*

—Saint Ambrose, "Our Comforting Lord"

# Fear About Your Emotional State

Sometimes, as we go through the normal grieving ups and downs, we begin to worry that we can't handle it, that we're going crazy, or that we're not recovering as we should. These worries are normal, but they're generally unfounded.

When Nancy's husband was diagnosed with amyotrophic lateral sclerosis, also known as Lou Gehrig's disease, she was completely devastated. Once a robust man, he was gradually debilitated by the disease.

Nancy's grieving really began with the diagnosis. At first, she was numb, in shock. Her husband kept working as a carpenter, and neither of them wanted to admit what was ahead. But before long he couldn't grasp a hammer, and then he needed a wheelchair.

There were times of anger—at the disease, at the doctors, at God—and time spent grasping at miracle cures. Then finally, two years after the diagnosis, he was gone, and Nancy plunged into the grieving process again. But after another year, she seemed to have regained a certain equilibrium. Except for those occasional reminders. "Our anniversary was a hard time," says Nancy. "Sometimes just seeing his chair in the living room would make me cry. Or I would slip back after hearing a song that was ours."

Some experts call it "the slippery slope." Just when you think you've licked one stage and moved on to the next, you slip back. And even after you've "recovered," you will probably be surprised and dismayed by some backward lapses. Where did that come from? Do I have to go through all of that again?

No, you don't. For years after your loss, you can expect to flashback momentarily to stages you thought you were finished with. It doesn't mean you're crazy. It means you're normal.

Of course, these flashes of sadness or anger or temptation can still be quite frightening.

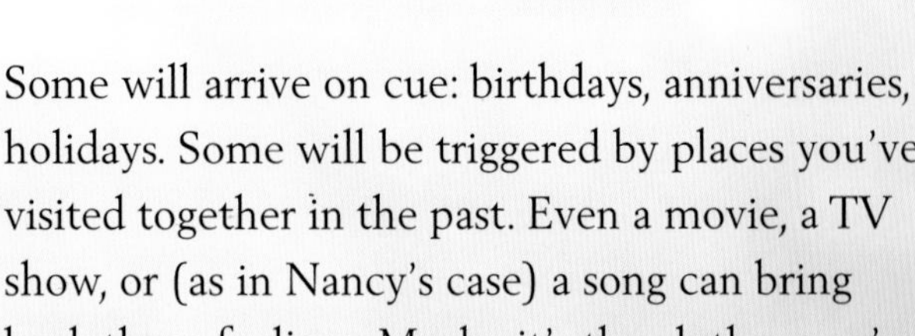

Some will arrive on cue: birthdays, anniversaries, holidays. Some will be triggered by places you've visited together in the past. Even a movie, a TV show, or (as in Nancy's case) a song can bring back those feelings. Maybe it's the clothes you're wearing that your loved one bought for you.

In all these cases, the memories trigger something else, some unfinished business. For a moment, perhaps, you need to go back into denial and pretend that your loved one is still nearby. Or maybe you focus on some regret or some issue you never resolved with that person.

A widow might be going through her finances a year after her husband's death and suddenly blurt out in anger, "Why didn't you keep records of these investments?" She might be stunned by her own vehemence, but it's not really about record keeping. It's about the anger that's still buried within her. She really means to say, "Why did you die? I'm still hurting because you left." It's good to get those feelings out. Chances are, she's not plunging back into a three-month anger jag. It's just a droplet left in the pipeline. It needed to trickle out.

On the third anniversary of a child's death, a man might go to a bar and get drunk. It's a quick-fix strategy, a way to escape the pain, but it's something he stopped doing years ago. Why this relapse? After all this time, he thought the pain was behind him. But now, it is as fresh as if the death just happened. Apparently his painful memories caught him at a weak moment. Chances are, he'll realize that this bender doesn't really fix anything. He'll pick himself up, dust himself off, and continue forward.

In Psalm 23, we read about walking through "the darkest valley." In a way, that's the bereavement process—a long walk through a dark valley. And it is the shadow of death—the death of our loved one—that looms over us, blocking the light, keeping us from seeing a clear path.

At various points along the way—Denial Bluff, Anger Canyon, the Quick-Fix Quicksand, or the Pit of Depression—the terrain is difficult. We fear we might get stuck. And even when we think we're free and clear, we find ourselves under that shadow again from time to time. It's just part of the process.

"I fear no evil," the psalmist says, "for you are with me" (23:4). The Lord is shepherding us through that recovery process. Step by step, and even through our relapses, he will keep moving us forward. He gives us the courage to keep putting one foot in front of the other.

*Rock of my Salvation,*

*Free me from fear. Give me the courage I need to get through each day. My heart feels raw, as if it could burst at any moment. But I don't want to go through life on eggshells. I want to live boldly. I want to dance. But fear holds me back. Keep letting me know you are right there beside me. Keep leading me down the path you have set for me. Amen.*

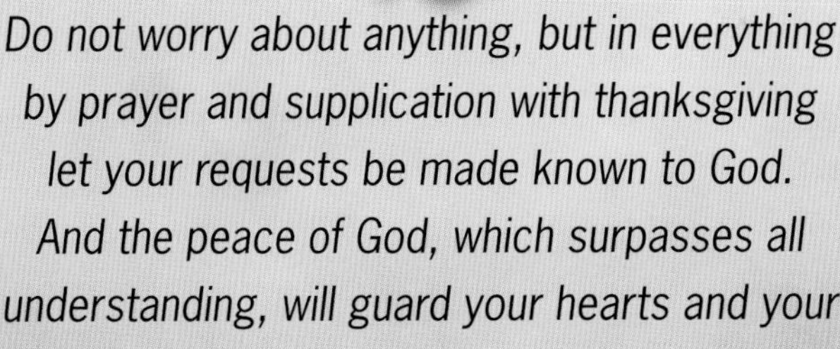

Do not worry about anything, but in everything by prayer and supplication with thanksgiving let your requests be made known to God. And the peace of God, which surpasses all understanding, will guard your hearts and your minds in Christ Jesus.

—Philippians 4:6–7

# What to Do About Fears and Worries

We've been discussing various "times" in the grieving process, and our general approach is that they happen. You will go through these periods as you need to, and they will last as long as they need to. Your emotions are making certain adjustments along the way, and eventually you'll move on.

Your "strategy," then, is to make efficient use of these times. Let them do their work, but don't get stuck in their unhealthy aspects. This is especially true in our times of fear and worry. Is there anything good about fear and worry? Sure! We've already seen how an appropriate level of concern can motivate us to help children or those closest to the deceased. It might also be that a sudden fear of death, brought on by a friend's untimely demise, might kick-start some young slacker into making something of his or her life.

One writer has distinguished between manipulative fear and motivating fear. That's a helpful distinction. Manipulative fear keeps you from doing important things. It twists your view of yourself and your future to make you expect the worst. But motivating fear drives you into action. It helps you make important choices, because you're well aware of the danger if you don't.

***Use the positive motivation of your fears and worries.*** What specifically are you worried about? Write it down and evaluate it. Are there things you could do to improve the situation, for yourself or others?

***Avoid the negative manipulation of your fears and worries.*** As you evaluate your list of fears, sort through what's valid and what's not. Look for areas where you've been paralyzed, unable to act because fear is holding you back. Get a realistic idea of what you could do in those situations.

***Get some nonworriers on your support team.*** You need to surround yourself with people who act rather than worry. Yes, you will always have some worriers around you, but find advisers who aren't consumed by fear.

***Pray and listen.*** One of the most common phrases in scripture is "Fear not." Let God's peace wash over you. Don't just go through some rote prayer each day. Take some extra time to listen. If there are worries flooding your mind, lay them out before the Lord and ask what he wants you to do with them.

*You will not fear the terror of the night, or the arrow that flies by day, or the pestilence that stalks in darkness, or the destruction that wastes at noonday.*

—Psalm 91:5–6

*Almighty God,*

*Protect me from my own crazy emotions. These days I don't know whether I'm coming or going. I'm angry, depressed, and oddly optimistic, all in the same day. I'm confusing my friends and terrifying myself. It's like I have no control over how I feel. And just when I think I'm moving on, getting over it, ready to start my life anew—wham!—I get blindsided by some new emotion. Am I going crazy? I don't think so, but it sure feels that way.*

*Lord, save me from all this. You're the only one who can. Amen.*

Chapter 8

# Times of Spiritual Challenge

***Grief often brings us into an important time of spiritual reformatting.***

Whenever you face trials of any kind, consider it nothing but joy, because you know that the testing of your faith produces endurance; and let endurance have its full effect, so that you may be mature and complete.

—James 1:2–4

# Testing Our Belief

"I am sixty years old and for the first time during all these long years, so far as memory serves me, has God in his infinite mercy allowed me to have any sorrow that I could not cast on him."

The writer of those words was William Booth, founder of the Salvation Army. His wife lay dying, and he couldn't understand why. Booth was a man of great faith. His preaching had brought challenge and comfort to thousands, but watching his beloved Catherine ebb away was "an experience of sorrow, which words can but poorly describe." He tried to go about his daily routine, rising at six, working for two hours before breakfast, but still he found himself breaking down in tears, moaning, "How can it be? How can it be?"

Maybe you are experiencing a similar grief. Along with the sorrow comes the question:

"Why, God, why?" This usually makes the sorrow worse. At the very moment when you need to "cast your care" on your comforting Lord, you find yourself nurturing deep suspicions about his intentions. How could he let this happen?

Many people have an intellectual curiosity about this question. If God is all-loving and God is all-powerful, then how could he allow painful events to occur in our lives? Philosophers have considered this problem in one volume after another, but when a crisis hits home, suddenly it's more than a mental exercise. When we lose someone precious, it's an emotional issue. It quickly becomes a spiritual challenge. We tend to feel that God has betrayed us. And that creates another major loss in our lives—a loss of intimacy with our Creator, perhaps even a loss of faith.

*Be still, and know that I am God!*

—Psalm 46:10

# Feeling Betrayed

What do we do with that feeling of betrayal? People usually go in one of two directions. Some find their faith shattered. If they've trusted God to protect them and their loved ones from pain and harm, then they've been disappointed, to say the least. They feel that God has proven untrustworthy. Why should they continue to worship a God who either cannot help or doesn't care?

This is strong language, to be sure, but these are strong feelings. After losing a loved one, many people get very angry with God, and they take it out on him by shutting him out of their lives. No more church. No more Bible. What's the use?

The other direction is more pious but less honest. People feel hurt by God, but they don't want to admit that. They don't want to be disrespectful, so they don't tell God how they really feel. They pretend to continue in their faith, as if nothing happened—but their faith has actually been severely jolted. They end up holding a grudge against God and remaining very distant. It's sort of like that uncle who owes you money but won't pay up. You see him at family functions, and you might even say hello in a terse, formal way, but there's a distance between you.

Both of these directions are understandable options. When your world has turned upside down, it's only natural to reappraise your faith. But there is a better way.

***As you know, God, my spirit has been anything but gentle lately. I've been wracked with questions, tormented by doubts, burning with anger. I long for your peace. Grant me your peace. Breathe into my life your gentle peace. Amen.***

# The Sufferer

The book of Job raises questions about faith. It starts out with a wager between God and the devil. God is actually bragging about Job's faith, and Satan suggests that it's only because God takes such good care of him. Job was, after all, a rich rancher with a large family. Why wouldn't he trust the God who gave all this to him?

So God agrees to let Satan take away Job's wealth and his family, and ultimately even his health. Despite all that, Job refuses to curse God. His own wife mocks him on her way out the door, but Job responds, "Shall we receive the good at the hand of God, and not receive the bad?" (Job 2:10).

Job has three friends, and later a fourth, who come over and sit with him in his sorrow. The bulk of the book consists of their attempts to explain his suffering. Generally, they suggest that he must have done something to deserve his suffering. Why else would God allow this to happen? Job doggedly maintains his innocence.

Finally God himself speaks, and we perk up, expecting answers. Instead, he brings more questions. "Can you make an ocean?" he asks. "I can." In highly poetic language, he surveys his creation. "Can you make a hippopotamus? I can. You see those stars? I put them there." This is a loose paraphrase, of course, but the gist of God's argument is this: "I'm God, and you're not."

**I would rather walk with God in the dark than go alone in the light.**

**—Mary Gardiner Brainard**

As Frederick Buechner put it: "God doesn't explain. He explodes. . . . God doesn't reveal his grand design. He reveals himself." There's wisdom in that approach. As we look back over the book of Job, we realize that it's not really about suffering; it's about faith in the midst of suffering. The wager is based on Job's faith. And what is Job's faith based on?

Well, if it was based on a set of answers to theological questions, he would be in trouble.

That was apparently the situation with Job's friends—at least the first three. They trusted in their idea of how God should run things: good rewards for good behavior, consequences for bad behavior. That makes a lot of sense, and many people today share that basic idea. But God rises above that level. He refuses to be boxed in by our sense of what he should and shouldn't do. He keeps surprising us. After all, he's God and we're not.

Grief comes in seasons. The cold numbness of autumn blows through the soul as we grope to accept what has happened. The fall gives way to the dark despair of winter when the sun refuses to shine. But then we witness the first glimmer of spring, and our hearts begin to feel a little lighter. Hope spreads like sunshine, and we bloom under its warmth, where before we were withered and deadened. We breathe again, and fresh air fills our hungry lungs. We bask in the glow of summer, grateful to be alive.

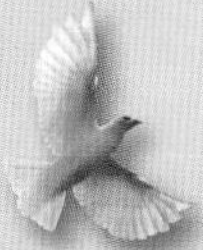

*Drop thy still dews of quietness,*
*Till all our strivings cease;*
*Take from our souls the strain and stress,*
*And let our ordered lives confess*
*Thy beauty of thy peace.*

—John Greenleaf Whittier, "The Brewing of Soma"

# Finding His Peace

As we go through our times of spiritual challenge, we might find a whole lot of shaking going on. Some of our assumptions about life and about God may crumble as we're forced to determine what is truly worth believing in.

So, what is your faith based on? Are you trusting in God or a set of ideas about God? Are you trusting in the Creator of all, whose ways are higher than your ways, whose thoughts are higher than your thoughts (Isaiah 55:9)? What kind of God would he be if he fit into our boxes?

If your faith has been shattered, or at least challenged, by the sorrowful events of the past—maybe that's a good thing. Maybe some of your ideas about God need to be reshaped. Maybe it's an opportunity to consider how great and awesome God is, how far beyond our expectations he resides.

Does this mean that God doesn't love us? Not at all. But he certainly loves us in ways we don't always understand. A child may misunderstand a parent's intentions: *I have to leave my playmates and come inside for dinner? Now? You don't love me anymore!* Of course that's far from the truth. The parent loves the child in ways that are higher than the child's understanding.

Does this mean that God is always distant and awe-inspiring, rather than close and comforting? Not at all. God draws near to us in our need. He promises peace.

The apostle Paul was in prison when he wrote to the believers at Philippi, "Do not worry about anything, but in everything by prayer and supplication with thanksgiving let your requests be made known to God. And the peace of God, which surpasses all understanding, will guard your hearts and your minds in Christ Jesus" (Philippians 4:6–7).

Prayer is a cure for anxiety. The God who made the universe—oceans and hippopotamuses and stars—wants to hear about our problems. When we turn our anxieties, our frustrations, and our sorrows over to him, he gives us peace. But notice how he describes this peace. It "surpasses all understanding."

You might never understand why. Your questions might bubble up forever. As we saw in the case of Job, God tends not to give answers. But he does give himself. He brings his awesome, surprising presence into your life and wraps you up in his peace.

**For the mountains may depart and the hills be removed, but my steadfast love shall not depart from you, and my covenant of peace shall not be removed, says the Lord, who has compassion on you.**

**—Isaiah 54:10**

As he prepared to leave his disciples, Jesus said something similar. "Peace I leave with you; my peace I give to you. I do not give to you as the world gives. Do not let your hearts be troubled, and do not let them be afraid" (John 14:27). Notice again: His peace is not "as the world gives." People might expect answers to all questions. They might expect wealth and pleasure in reward for faithfulness. They might expect believers to get a free ride on matters of suffering. That's the world's kind of peace, but the Lord's peace is different. He sees us through our hard times. We don't need to have troubled hearts, not because we're immune from trouble but because God is with us. We rest in him, and he grants us peace.

*In all human sorrows nothing gives comfort but love and faith.*

—Leo Tolstoy, *Anna Karenina*

In the depth of my pain, I cry out to God. In grief and sorrow, in loss and anguish, I cry out to God. When I am overwhelmed and cannot bear another moment, I cry out to God. And he hears my cry. He listens and cares and answers, as he always has throughout all time.

# A Dark Cloud

There are still times of deep sadness and depression. But there is something holding us up through those difficulties. God's presence becomes the bedrock of our lives.

Jonathan Edwards was probably the most famous man in colonial America. Respected as a scholar, revered as a pastor, he finally reached the peak of his profession at age 54, when he was asked to serve as president of Princeton University (then known as the College of New Jersey). He left the pastorate of his Massachusetts church to assume this prestigious post. His wife, Sarah, was going to wrap things up at home and join him in New Jersey a few months later.

At least that was the plan. Just a few weeks into his new job, before Sarah could join him, Jonathan came down with smallpox. As he lay dying, he dictated this message: "Give my kindest love to my dear wife and tell her that the uncommon union that has so long subsisted between us has been . . . spiritual and therefore will continue forever. And I hope she will be supported under so great a trial and submit cheerfully to the will of God. And as to my children, you are now . . . left fatherless, which I hope will be an inducement to you to seek a Father who will never fail you."

One of his grown daughters, who lived in New Jersey, was at his bedside. But he would never see his wife and other children again. At least not on this side of eternity. His last words of wisdom to his daughter were: "Trust in God and you do not need to be afraid."

As you would expect, Sarah took the news hard. Not only was there the shock of losing her husband and the grief involved with that, but her mind was flooded with questions. Why would God lead Jonathan to this faraway job, only to let him die before he could get anything done? Surely Jonathan had more good work to do on this earth. Why would God take him now? It just didn't make sense.

In the following weeks and months, she continued to wrestle with this issue. A woman of great faith, she didn't want to doubt God's goodness, but it was hard to trust in him after what had happened. Jonathan was well known for preaching about God's sovereignty, and Sarah had often helped him plan his sermons and writings. So we can assume that she thoroughly understood the theology of a God who is completely in charge, a God who can do whatever he wants. But that might have made it even harder for her to grasp this situation. Why would God do this to her?

Two weeks after Jonathan's death, Sarah wrote to one of her children: "What shall I say? A holy and good God has covered us with a dark cloud." She credits the goodness of God for the fact that "we had him so long." And in the midst of her sorrow, she adds, "But my God lives, and he has my heart. Oh, what a legacy my husband and your father has left us. We are all given to God and there I am and love to be."

It's never easy. The death of a loved one puts anyone into an emotional and spiritual jumble.

Sarah Edwards admitted that her life was covered with "a dark cloud," but she reaffirmed her faith in a "holy and good God." You might not be so articulate, and you don't have to be. We saw the same sort of jumble in the psalms, great faith interspersed with bitter complaints and cries for help. *Where are you? Help me! Why do you allow this? I praise you. I need you. Thank you.* In the throes of grief, that emotional roller-coaster ride is to be expected.

"My tears have been my food day and night," one psalmist complains, "while people say to me continually, 'Where is your God?'" Later in the same composition, he asks God, "Why have you forgotten me?" (Psalm 42:3, 9).

Many believers feel hesitant to give voice to these questions, but there they are in the Bible! Even Jesus exclaimed from the cross, "My God, my God, why have you forsaken me?" (Matthew 27:46). There's nothing wrong with asking such questions—just don't let that be the end of the conversation. Jesus went on to say, "Father, into your hands I commend my spirit" (Luke 23:46). And, as we've seen, the psalmist keeps us guessing. Taunted by his enemies, feeling totally forgotten by God, he does a bit of self-analysis. "Why are you cast down, O my soul, and why are you disquieted within me? Hope in God; for I shall again praise him, my help and my God" (Psalm 42:11). He's honest about his current state of mind, but he knows the final chapter hasn't been written yet.

Prayer is the burden of a sigh,
The falling of a tear,
The upward glancing of an eye
When none but God is near.

—James Montgomery

*Lord, forgive me for forgetting. I know you're with me always. You have said it in a hundred Bible verses. "Fear not, for I am with you." Even in the "valley of the shadow of death," you are with me. I know all that, but I forget to look for you. I cry out in pain as if no one's listening, but you are right there beside me. You do care about me.*

*So, I'm sorry for my selective memory. I trust in your forgiveness. Amen.*

# Where Is He?

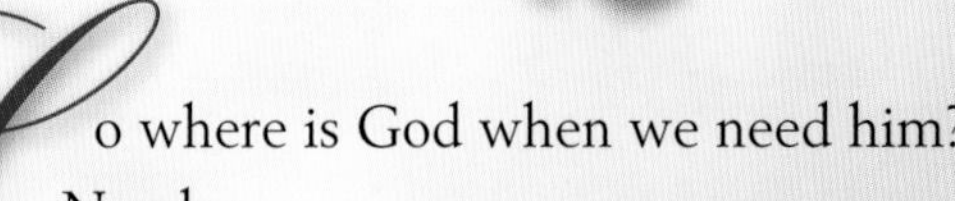

So where is God when we need him?

Nearby.

He's like a dad teaching a kid to ride a bike. For a while he runs alongside, his hands firmly on the bike and the child. But at a certain point the hands come off, and the child rides alone. Where's Dad? Close behind, watching, maybe praying, ready to rush in if needed.

Or consider the toddler racing down the aisle in a supermarket. It's all about her feet, her new shoes, her teetering balance, and all the cool stuff on the bottom shelves. But suddenly she stops and looks around. Where's Mom? Suddenly her sense of adventure is replaced by paralyzing fear. Of course Mom is only a few steps away, moving in quickly to scoop up the crying youngster. But those few seconds seem like forever in the child's young experience. And the tears are as much about anger as fear. "Where were you, Mom? Why weren't you there when I needed you? You left me out there, all alone, for four, maybe even five seconds! How could you?"

We do the same sort of thing with God. We feel abandoned in a time of great need. We're afraid and angry. But the truth is, he's right there with us. We may not recognize him right away. He might be allowing us to move out on our own a little, but he's never far.

**The Lord is near to all who call on him, to all who call on him in truth.**
**—Psalm 145:18**

"Do not fear," the Lord said through Isaiah, "for I am with you, do not be afraid, for I am your God; I will strengthen you, I will help you, I will uphold you with my victorious right hand" (Isaiah 41:10). The author of Hebrews seconded this motion. "For he has said, 'I will never leave you or forsake you'" (Hebrews 13:5).

It is part of God's nature to be with us. In the garden of Eden, God came looking for Adam and Eve even after they had sinned (Genesis 3:9). In a time of national threat, God gave Isaiah a specific message to console his people. In Isaiah 7:14, he

says a child would be born with the Hebrew title Immanuel, which means "God is with us." That prophecy was later applied to the birth of Jesus, who was called the Word (of God) that "became flesh and lived among us" (John 1:14).

God has never chosen to be a distant overlord who winds up his creation and lets it run on its own. The entire Bible is the record of his involvement with his people. He acts in human history. He talks with people. He motivates people to make a difference. He longs for a deeper relationship with humankind. Yes, there have been times when Moses or David or Jeremiah wondered where God had gone. Situations had grown so bad that the Lord seemed absent. But the truth, as they eventually acknowledged, was that God was never far away.

*Lord God,*

*"I am not skilled to understand what God has willed, what God has planned."*

*I can relate to the words of that old hymn because I don't get it. Maybe if I had a theology degree I could figure something out, but honestly I'm clueless. I do not have the skill to understand why you would allow such pain and grief in my life.*

*I trust you. I'm trying to trust you more. Can you help me out on this? Amen.*

# God of Suffering

In times of suffering, it's common to think that God has abandoned us, but the Bible gives us a different story. For some reason, God has chosen to be a sufferer too. The prophet Hosea details his own suffering at the hands of an unfaithful wife, but it's clear that his woes are mirroring the suffering of God, whose people chase after false gods. "The more I called them, the more they went from me; they kept . . . offering incense to idols," the Lord complained (Hosea 11:2).

Isaiah prophesied about a servant who would arise, but he would be "despised and rejected" and "a man of suffering" (Isaiah 53:3). The New Testament identifies Jesus as this servant. "By his wounds you have been healed," says Peter, quoting directly from Isaiah (1 Peter 2:24).

In that same passage, Peter speaks to slaves who suffered at the hands of unjust masters and

Christians who suffered for their faith, suggesting that they were "called" to suffer like this—"because Christ also suffered for you, leaving you an example, so that you should follow in his steps" (v. 21).

Where is God when we are suffering emotionally from the loss of a loved one? He is suffering along with us. He is inviting us into his heart. Perhaps as we go through these difficult times in our lives, we'll understand more fully the feelings of our God.

*Yes, I have doubted. I have wandered off the path. I have been lost. But I always returned. It is beyond the logic I seek. It is intuitive—an intrinsic, built-in sense of direction. I seem always to find my way home. My faith has wavered but has saved me.*

—Helen Hayes

Chapter 9

# Times of Impatience

***When will the grieving end? Part of you is ready to be done with it and get on with life, but the other part still needs to heal.***

He gives power to the faint,
and strengthens the powerless. . . .
but those who wait for the Lord
shall renew their strength,
they shall mount up with wings like
eagles, they shall run and not be
weary, they shall walk and not faint.

—Isaiah 40:29, 31

# It's Been Over a Year

"How long will I feel this way?" Amanda wonders. "I'm tired of being so lonely!" Her frustration is palpable. A year-and-a-half after losing her mom, she is still aching. It doesn't help that she lives alone, works at home, and has had a few other emotional crises in the last 18 months. She's ready to be healthy again. Except she isn't.

Sixteen months after her husband died, Millie asked her counselor, "Why am I not getting over this?"

"What makes you think you're not getting over this?" he responded.

"I'm angry all the time. I just thought I'd be past this by now."

"Why do you expect to get through this any quicker?"

Counselors love to turn questions around like that, but this wasn't just a word game. Millie was tired of the recovery process, she wanted to be "cured," she worried that her slip-ups were dragging her back, and she suspected that she was unusually slow to get back to normal.

The counselor was just questioning what "normal" meant to her. Part of Millie's frustration came from some standard in her mind that she was not meeting. *Normal people recover in a year; what's wrong with me?*

But the truth is that every recovery is different. Everyone has unique needs and makes unique choices. People are functioning in different environments. They have different people around them, different extraneous issues. Early in the recovery process, a person's needs are great. They need to grieve. They need to remember. They need to protest this terrible event. They need to honor the one they've lost. But then there's a reconfiguration necessary. They need to rebuild their lives, making a series of choices—in their own way, in their own time.

In Millie's case, she knew that there were several steps that would speed her recovery. She could get a job. She could reconnect with her

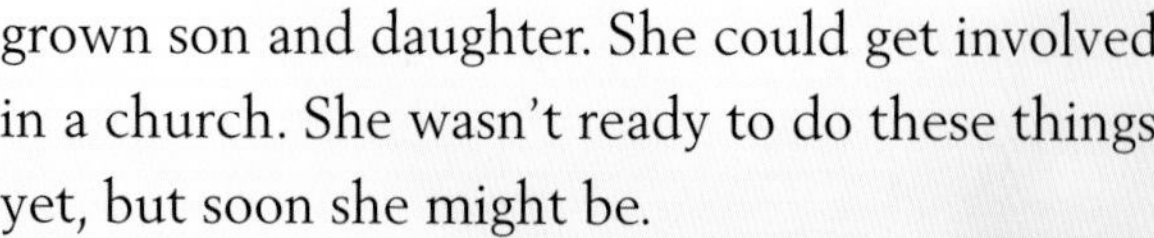

grown son and daughter. She could get involved in a church. She wasn't ready to do these things yet, but soon she might be.

This is what the counselor was driving at with his echoing questions. He could give her an agenda: *Do these three things, and call me in the morning.* But that wouldn't help if she wasn't ready for those actions. She needed to get to the point where her impatience exceeded her hesitations.

"I'm afraid to go into the job market. It's all new to me. I've never been on my own. My husband did all the finances for us. I wouldn't know what to do. . . . My son and daughter are focusing on their own spouses and kids. They don't need me poking my nose in their business. . . . I don't feel right about going back to church because I'm still upset with God. He took a good man."

Millie knows the way forward. She just can't go there yet. But maybe tomorrow she can. The counselor is gently pointing out that it's really up to her. Her impatience might be a good thing, in that it nudges her to make some courageous choices.

Left alone now, we drift aimlessly like untied balloons let loose to fly helter-skelter. Give us good sense to put off until tomorrow what we shouldn't try today. Reassure us this is temporary, a brief hesitation, not a giving up; hold up a mirror for us to see a once-again-clear-eyed person.

*God of all comfort,*

*I miss this dear one I've lost. I've been through the questions and tears. I know all things work together, but now it just comes down to missing. I want them here with me now. I miss them, and now it feels like a piece of me is missing.*

*Make me whole again. Bring comfort to my heart. Amen.*

# It Takes as Long as It Takes

"Grief can be very organic," says the Rev. Charles R. Mitchell, lead spiritual support counselor with Samaritan Health Care and Hospice. "You move at your own pace."

Not only will your rebuilding happen at your own pace, but the life you rebuild may be somewhat different from the life you had before. "Grief builds things back differently," Mitchell says. "You're finding a *new* normal."

In some ways, grief recovery is like recovering from an illness or injury—but it's not entirely the same. Yes, we experience downtime when we're sick, it might take a while to recover, during which time we're not functioning at full capacity. All of that is true with grief too. But when we finally recover from an illness, we're generally "as good as new." We get back to our lives as they were before the illness. That isn't the case with grief recovery. It doesn't just get us back to where we were before. It's a whole new adventure for us.

In *A Grief Observed,* C. S. Lewis wrote, "Grief is like a long valley, a winding valley where any bend may reveal a totally new landscape." He talked about the surprises we find, but this isn't just sentimental puffery. Always a bit of a cynic, Lewis admitted that sometimes the recovery process makes you feel like you're wandering around a "circular trench," but you're not. You are getting somewhere. It's just not always clear *where* that somewhere is.

A fire destroyed a family's nice suburban house. They came home from work to find it smoldering. They lost everything—clothing, furniture, and many irreplaceable keepsakes. They stayed with family and friends for a while, and their church pitched in to provide food and clothing. Eventually, with the insurance settlement and their own savings, they were able to build an even nicer house than the one they had lost.

The recovery process is something like that. You have lost something you can never replace. You will always feel sad about that. And for a while, you feel rootless, unattached. Friends are helping you out in your time of extreme need. But you are rebuilding—not the same life you had before, but a good life nonetheless.

Only by moving through the pain do we get to embrace the gift of healing and call it our own.

*Once, in my imagination I was taken down to the bed of the sea, and saw there green hills and dales that seemed to be clothed with moss, seaweed and stones. And I understood that if a person firmly believes that God is always with man, then even if he is thrown into the depths of the sea, he will be preserved in body and soul, and will enjoy greater solace and comfort than all this world can offer.*

—Julian of Norwich, *Revelations of Divine Love*

When the despair that comes with the pain of a loss immobilizes us and makes us feel powerless, God gives us the inner fortitude and grace we need to get up, get over the suffering, and get on with our lives. But let us remember to be patient with ourselves. We need to allow the grief to work through us so we can heal.

# Managing the Mess

So, how should you handle your life in the meantime? You're healing, but you're not yet whole. You're on your way somewhere, but you're not sure where that is. You're frustrated and impatient because you can see some kind of normalcy in front of you, but each day you get pulled back into grief.

It might help to think of your "life management" on three fronts: Feelings, Things, and Relationships.

***Feelings.*** Here's the key to managing your feelings as you move along in your recovery: *Don't.* A lot of people feel pressure to *seem* like they're doing better. "I can't burst into tears now. What will everyone think?" As a result, they hold back the passing wave of sorrow, and it hurts them eventually. That is, it stalls the healing process.

They try so hard to appear that they're further along in the process that they actually slip back.

Emotions need to come out. You have plenty of them right now, and they're unpredictable. You're a little scared of them. But you still need to feel what you feel. Don't set yourself back in your impatient attempt to be "all better." Let your feelings be what they are. "Tears are a gift from God," says counselor Mitchell. "Tears articulate how we feel when we can't use words."

Words are good too. Talk through your feelings with your closest friends. Those who love you best will take the time to listen to you. You might be afraid that you're just spouting a jumble of incoherent ramblings, but it's therapeutic to talk about these things. "You get to a point where you think people don't want to hear about it, but they do," said one mourner.

**All human wisdom is summed up in two words: wait and hope.**

**—Alexandre Dumas, *The Count of Monte Cristo***

Obviously, you are still responsible for your actions. "Letting your feelings out" doesn't mean punching out the clerk at the convenience store because you happened to be feeling anger at that moment. And you might have moments in your life when you choose not to cry—at work, perhaps, or leading a group, or tending children, or in the grocery store. But whenever that happens, you incur a debt you need to pay, soon. If you hold back your emotions for the moment, find another moment to go off by yourself to have a good cry or to punch a pillow or to wail at the top of your lungs.

So, yes, you can manage the *expression* of your feelings, but don't try to squelch the feelings themselves. They need to be what they will be.

***Things.*** "There are things in my home that remind me of my mother," said Amanda. "When I see them, it's like a knife in my heart. And I wonder: Is it better to take those things away so I don't have those five seconds of pain or to leave them out so I can remember her? I'm not sure."

There's no right answer here. Or, more precisely, no wrong answer. Pain and memory seem to go together at this point in recovery. One is desirable; the other isn't.

In a grief support group, one man says his wife's clothing is still in the closet, 16 months after her death. He just can't bear to get rid of it. Another man says, "The week after her death, my wife's sisters cleaned all of her stuff out of our bedroom, all her personal things. It was the best thing they could have done for me."

We feel a connection to people through the things they used, the gifts they gave us, the items they cherished. It feels as if we have a little piece of them with us—a physical, tangible piece. There's nothing wrong with this. You might want to keep mementos of your loved one forever.

But there also might be great symbolic value in putting some of those items aside, giving them away. If you get to the point where you want to tell yourself—to *show* yourself—that you're committed to moving forward, not backward, you might find it helpful to get rid of the objects that are shackling you to the memories of those you've lost. This is your call, entirely. There's no problem with holding onto these things, but there could be some value in freeing yourself from them.

**Let this be your comfort: You are not the first to walk in the fearful path nor will you be the last. But each traveler is precious to God and walks under his watchful eye.**

So the guy with his wife's clothing still in the closet after 16 months—he might say, "I could use that closet space for my hockey equipment now that I'm hitting the ice again, and maybe some charity could make good use of those dresses." That would be a good step forward for him, when he's ready.

A personal anecdote from the author of this book: I lost a dear friend last year, and her family gave me her impressive collection of books. I donated many to local libraries and added some to my own library. Among the books were a few empty spiral-bound notebooks, since she loved to write, as do I. Well, as I rushed out the door to interview a grief counselor for this book, I grabbed a notebook from the shelf. Halfway through the interview, I realized this was one of her notebooks—and I had to smile. Was there a better way for me to use her stuff? Her death shook me, and her memory inspires me. Now her notebook helped me as I try to help others deal with their own crises of death and memory.

Maybe you can find a wonderfully appropriate, creative way to honor the memory of the one you've lost as you use the things they've left behind.

***Relationships.*** Counselors report a recurring phenomenon. Men who have lost their wives show up at a grief support group one time, and sometime during the session they ask, "Is it too

soon to start dating again?" They get a noncommittal answer—there's no timetable, it's your unique process, your emotional journey, etc.—and they never show up again. The counselors assume they're too busy dating.

Hank was an older man who had lost his wife of many years. He grieved deeply for a few months, but then he met a woman at the facility where he lived. He fell madly in love and wanted to marry her. Maybe unfortunately for him, his son was a psychologist.

"You asked for my professional opinion. I'm giving it to you. Don't do it. You're asking for trouble."

"But I miss being married."

"You're just looking for someone to replace Mom, to do the things she did. You can't replace Mom, ever. Any new relationship has to grow on its own, and that takes time."

As it happened, Hank went ahead and remarried, and the new marriage was contentious. Soon Hank was complaining to his son about how he and his new wife fought all the time.

If you are a widow or widower, there may come a time when you can forge a new romance and remarry, but don't rush things. Go into any new relationship with your eyes wide open. A new marriage would be a whole new thing, quite apart from what you had before, and yet

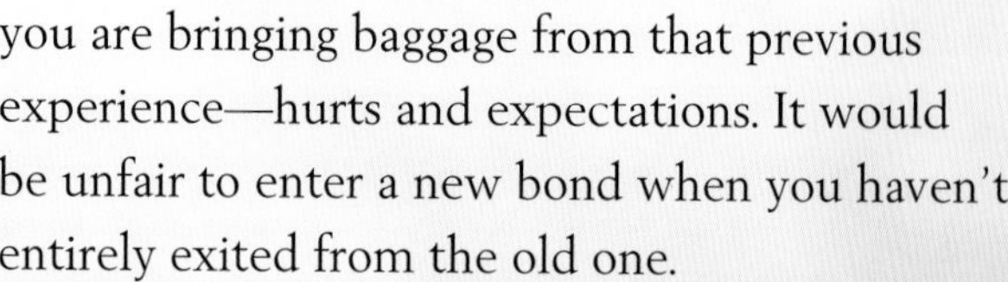

you are bringing baggage from that previous experience—hurts and expectations. It would be unfair to enter a new bond when you haven't entirely exited from the old one.

But that's the problem with impatience. You think you're ready. You want to be ready. You tell yourself your new relationship will heal anything that still needs healing. But that's not true. A new relationship, no matter how loving it is, will add complications to your life, which will likely slow down or derail your healing process.

This is not only true for those who have lost their spouse. Any bereavement creates a sense of deep need, and often people rush into romantic relationships to meet those needs. That is dangerous and counterproductive.

You are likely to find some amazing friends in your recovery process. These are the people who prove their mettle by being there for you, listening to you, caring for you, without promise of reward. You may form relationships with these people that can last far into the future—as dear friends, and perhaps someday as a mate. Just don't wreck everything by jumping too soon.

*Lord,*

*Just help me hang on. Help me get through. Help me put one foot in front of the other. Help me do what I have to do for those who rely on me. I don't even know how I'm going to get through. I can't see past today's pain. I feel like giving up. But I trust you to help me. I trust you to give me the strength I need.*

*And it's all I can do to say Amen.*

Even in the midst of grieving, the mourner sooner or later begins to see little glimmers of hope. First an hour will go by when he does not think of his loss, then a few hours, then a day. Slowly, reconstruction begins.

—Billy Graham

# Friday Faith

The story is told of a preacher who stood up in church and said, "It's Friday, but Sunday's coming!" He got a few "Amens" from the faithful, and he repeated, "It's Friday, but Sunnnnday's coming!" The response got a little bigger, and he said it again.

Soon the whole church was rocking with "That's right" and "Hallelujah," as people caught on to his message. "It's Friday," he said, and the parishioners understood the tragedy of Jesus on the cross. "But Sunday's coming," and they knew the glory of the empty tomb was not far away. "It's Friday," he kept saying, and they saw the sadness of their own lives as the momentary grief of the disciples mourning the loss of their Lord. "But Sunnnnday is coming!" And they knew that there was a resurrection morning ahead for them as well.

As the story goes, that was the entire sermon in church that day, and it was surely the most memorable. Those listeners were reminded that God's specialty is turning tragedy to triumph, that our grimmest griefs are transformed into God's greatest glories.

David had a similar truth in mind as he penned Psalm 30. "O Lord my God, I cried to you for help, and you have healed me. O Lord, you . . . restored me to life from among those gone down to the Pit" (vs. 2–3).

Interesting choice of words there. In this book, we've talked about "the pit of depression," but for David, the Pit was death. He might be saying, "I almost died in battle, and you, Lord, saved my life." But this is a psalm about mourning, not about warfare. It's quite possible that he was mourning over the death of others and feeling a depression that was almost as if he himself were dying.

Before becoming king, David spent quite a while on the run from a jealous King Saul. One priest who helped David was later brutally murdered by Saul's forces. Perhaps David was mourning the loss of this courageous friend and feeling guilty about putting him in harm's way.

David's best friend was Jonathan, son of Saul. Both Saul and Jonathan died in the same battle, clearing the way for David to become king but causing him much sorrow as well.

As king, David had to fend off a revolt led by his own son Absalom. After his rebellious son died, David wept bitterly.

David also had an adulterous affair with Bathsheba, ordering her husband's death and conceiving a child with her. The prophet Nathan confronted David about the sin and predicted that the child would be stillborn. David publicly repented, clothing himself in ritual sackcloth, and he grieved for this loss.

Any one of these events could have sparked Psalm 30. David certainly knew about grief. "Weeping may linger for the night," he wrote, "but joy comes with the morning" (v. 5).

What's this? Joy? The psalms have a way of telling the beginning, middle, and end of a story all at once. In the following verses, David explains how his pride got him into trouble, how he cried out to the Lord, and how he tried to convince the Lord to come to his aid. But he blurts out the end of the story early—there is joy in the morning.

"You have turned my mourning into dancing," he added later. "You have taken off my sackcloth and clothed me with joy, so that my soul may praise you and not be silent" (vs. 11–12).

**God be praised, that to believing souls, gives light in darkness, comfort in despair.**

**—William Shakespeare**

David never downplayed his troubled times. This was not denial on his part. He knew what it was like to weep all night and weep the next night too. He faced more than his share of tragedy, some of which he brought on himself. But he understood that this story of grief had a happy ending. The night is long and difficult, but the day will dawn. And the new day will bring not only joy but dancing.

You may be in the middle of the grieving process. You might even be in that pit of depression. When you hear that joy comes with the morning, it might seem very far away. That's understandable. You don't need to do a joyful foxtrot yet; just know that it's in your future. It's still Friday for you, and you have plenty to grieve about. But Sunday's coming. And when that day dawns, you will dance.

Father, Mother, God. You who have made the moon and the stars and the sun. You who have given life its own rhythm and pattern. You who have instilled a divine order and timing to everything under the heavens. Make me resilient like the sandy beach upon which the waves crash. Make me strong like the mighty willow tree that bends but does not break in the high winds. Give me the patience and wisdom to know that my suffering will one day turn to a great understanding of your ways, your works, and your wonders.

*Help me understand, O God, that we can't have good without bad—a head without a tail. Help me remember the joy when grief strikes my heart. For just as it takes a negative to create a photograph, it takes darkness and light to complete creation. Therein lies the promise: Darkness is only half of the portrait of life.*

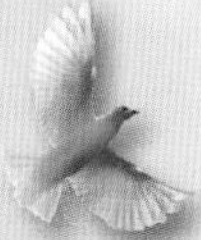

*Thank you, Lord, for reddened eyes. Believing your promise that comfort follows mourning, we bawl and sob. In your wisdom, onion-peeling salty tears differ from cleansing grieving ones; we're grateful for their healing. Deliver us from stiff upper lips, and if we've lost our tears, help us find them.*

*Chapter 10*

# Times of Connection with Others

***As you put your life back together, you may forge new relationships. It's not easy to care about a new friend when you've been wounded, but this is a path toward healing.***

Therefore encourage
one another and build up each other,
as indeed you are doing.

—1 Thessalonians 5:11

# A Hero Dies

"She's my hero," Jason said, introducing her to the congregation. At 60 years of age, Patricia had led a full life, and a hard life. She had served as a pastor, one of the first women ordained in her area. But she had a child with severe special needs, and when her husband took off, she had to focus on the child. Still, she remained involved in churches, offering them her creative service, humble love, and wry humor.

Jason worked on a big church staff and was temporarily assigned to provide the preaching for a tiny church nearby. If ten people showed up for worship, it was a good day. But the church had enjoyed a long history, had a quaint clapboard building, and dreamed of better days. So Jason preached there when he could and found replacements when he couldn't. Patricia was one of the replacements.

It soon became apparent that Patricia fit in very nicely. She seemed to understand the issues of a congregation going through tough times, and the people loved both Patricia and her daughter. Jason suggested that Patricia take on the pastorate of the church. Everyone agreed.

**This present sadness is so overwhelming that the rest of the story is forgotten, O God. Give me eyes of faith to read between the lines and see rebuilders, friends, and family, change and healing.**

Now he was occasionally filling in for her—and each time he did, he saw a slow, steady advancement in the church. A few more people at worship, but more importantly, a sense of hope, an understanding of their own value, a spiritual growth, even a creative spark that he credited to Patricia. She was Jason's hero, a person who continued to serve the Lord despite all her difficulties.

A phone call came to Jason one Thursday night. Patricia had died the previous night. Heart attack. Could he preach on Sunday? Well, yes, of course.

It was a shock. She had gone through heart surgery a few years earlier. Medically it wasn't a surprise, but she was so full of life. How could she be gone?

Funeral arrangements were made. Relatives were notified. People stepped up to care for her daughter. Jason needed to take care of the preaching not just this week, but for the next few months, and he was happy to commit to that. It was one way he could honor the memory of his hero.

And so Jason began preaching at this little church, to people who were in as much shock as he was. Many were elderly, no strangers to death, but there was still a pall of sadness in the place. Jason began preaching through the book of Acts, starting with the disciples wondering what to do now that Jesus was gone, waiting for what God would do next.

Jason would be the first to tell you that he doesn't do grief well. He sort of stuffs it deep, pretending it's not there. But somehow this was the perfect release for him, sharing the Bible with people who were grieving as he was, talking with them before and after the services, caring and being cared for. And slowly this community began to emerge from their sorrow. At first everyone was careful to do things exactly as Patricia had done. Then they began to develop some of the ideas Patricia had introduced. Finally they began to use their creativity, which Patricia had inspired, to set a course for the future.

After several months, the denomination appointed a new pastor. Jason says he will always look back to that time as an important one, when he learned about grief and he learned about community.

One of the most wonderful things about recovering from your grief is the help you get from other people. It's also one of the hardest.

**Father God, thank you for my many friends who stand beside me in all situations. They are always there when I need them to listen, laugh, and cry.**

Most people know very little about helping someone else through the loss of a loved one, but they still try hard to make things better. They mean well, they really do. (Keep telling yourself that.) But generally you wish they would just go away.

You may find, however, a few who are sensitive to your situation, who will listen to you rather than preach to you, who allow you to ask the tough questions and give you all the time you need to get from point A to point B. These people are precious. Thank them, bless them, honor them, and keep their phone numbers handy.

But not all connections are positive.

*Lord,*

*Thank you for all the precious people who have stood by me in my time of need. When I was in the pit of depression, they sat there with me. When I was too weepy to eat, they fed me. When I needed to cry out in grief and anger, they gave me pillows to punch and dishes to throw. And when I needed to remember, they brought out the photo album.*

*Their gifts have sustained me in my darkest hour, and I thank you, Lord, for working through them. Amen.*

Weep with those who weep.

—Romans 12:15

# Cheerleaders

Have you seen the musical *Annie?* Based on the long-running comic strip *Little Orphan Annie,* this story follows an abandoned child from the orphanage to the mansion of the richest man in the country, Daddy Warbucks. Annie tags along with him to a cabinet meeting at the White House, where President Roosevelt's advisors are moaning about the Great Depression.

It's a cute scene. These experts are worried about poverty and unemployment and war—and rightly so. It was a bleak time. Then Annie starts singing, "The sun'll come out tomorrow." Her optimism is a hard sell in this smoke-filled room, but soon it inspires the president. He forces his reluctant advisors to sing along with Annie about the beauty of "Tomorrow, Tomorrow."

The tide turns. Once the song is over, they all get back to work, but now they're looking at a bright future. The government could hire unemployed people, someone suggests, to do various projects that would keep America great. The ideas are flying fast and furious. FDR himself is agog at the possibilities. This is a new direction for the country, a way out of the doldrums. It's a New Deal.

**I lift up my eyes to the hills— from where will my help come?**
**—Psalm 121:1**

And so the plucky optimism of a red-haired orphan changed the course of history. At least that's how the musical goes.

You probably know some people like Annie. When everything's looking grim, they're crowing about maintaining a positive mental outlook. *Why so glum, chum? It will all work out,* they say. *Sure, you've had some hard times, but life will get better. Tomorrow's a new day. Cheer up.*

Chances are, those people really annoy you.

They mean well. They really do. But they're ignoring a major truth about our existence. Sometimes life hurts. It's like they're trying to slap a coat of bright, shiny paint over any smudge of pain or sorrow. Sometimes you even

## What to say

Sometimes you have to coach people on how to help you. They come along with advice, platitudes, Bible verses, but you just don't want to hear that. You know they mean well, but you need them to stop. What can you say? Adapt these to your particular situation.

- How am I doing? I'm surviving, day by day.
- Yes, things are hard, but I'm doing as well as can be expected.
- I appreciate your desire to help, but I need to find my own way right now. Please keep me in your prayers.
- Just come and sit with me a while. If I hear any more advice, I think I'll explode.
- You probably don't know what to say right now, and that's okay. Don't say anything. It's enough to know you care.
- Let's just go and do something fun, to take my mind off my troubles.
- I don't need answers right now, just a listening ear.
- Please be patient with me. I'm still grieving. I really can't take in all that you're saying.
- I know that God has a plan, but I'm not sure what that is right now, and I don't think you do either, so I'm just going to muddle around for a while and try to get through each day.
- I have a lot of questions and doubts right now that I need to sort through by myself.

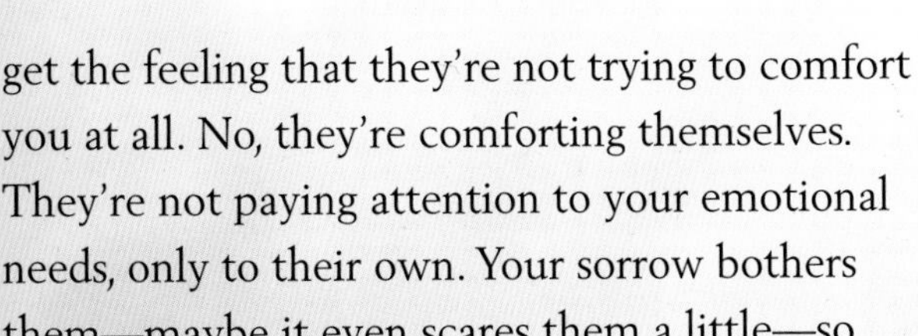

get the feeling that they're not trying to comfort you at all. No, they're comforting themselves. They're not paying attention to your emotional needs, only to their own. Your sorrow bothers them—maybe it even scares them a little—so they try to gloss over it. But you need to grieve.

The best comforters listen to you. They let you talk about how bad you feel. Yes, you need to talk about it sometimes. And there are other times when they'll sit with you in silence or share your tears. They may inject a note of hope every so often when you start despairing, but they're not about to burst into song. These people are gems. Treasure them. Keep them close beside you as you go through this difficult time. They may even help you fend off the annoying Annies of the world.

*Two are better than one. . . . if they fall,*
*one will lift up the other.*

—Ecclesiastes 4:9–10

*I'm in despair, God.*

*I'm in the black valley of hopelessness. Please remind me that you are there for me, even in my darkest hour. My loved one has left me. I know that person is now with you, but I still miss him.*

*My grief is sometimes overwhelming. Please help me remember that you are here with me.*

*In all my pain, I sometimes forget that you are here for me. Remind me of your love. Thank you, God. Amen.*

You grew weary from your many wanderings,
but you did not say, "It is useless."
You found your desire rekindled,
and so you did not weaken.

—Isaiah 57:10

The people God surrounds us with are making a difference in our lives and writing indelible lines on hearts, souls, and minds. We read in them God's message of grace and celebrate how far we've come.

*If then there is any encouragement in Christ, any consolation from love, any sharing in the Spirit, any compassion and sympathy, make my joy complete: be of the same mind, having the same love, being in full accord and of one mind. Do nothing from selfish ambition or conceit, but in humility regard others as better than yourselves. Let each of you look not to your own interests, but to the interests of others.*

—Philippians 2:1–4

# Lucky You

If you find yourself surrounded by would-be cheerleaders who won't rest until you're singing "Tomorrow" along with them, just smile and thank them for their good wishes. The problem is, you're in no condition to fight with them. You have a right to cry. You have a need to cry. You just don't have the energy to fight for it. They burst in with their perky pep talks, and what can you say? They seem to have the moral high ground. Sometimes they can even make you feel that you're unspiritual because you're not happy enough. When you're already feeling down, that can drive you even deeper into the pits.

But are they right? Doesn't God want us to "rejoice always"? Let's take a look at what Jesus had to say.

It was one of his first public statements, in a collection of sayings we know as the Beatitudes, at the beginning of the talk we call the Sermon on the Mount. The fact that this sermon appears in slightly different forms in the gospels of Matthew and Luke makes us think that Jesus preached it repeatedly. This is very important material.

"Blessed are . . ."

That's how he begins each of his first nine sentences. The word *blessed* here means happy, fortunate, even lucky. It's really not a very religious term. Who are the lucky people in this world? The rich? The powerful? Those adored by millions or just cherished by their own families? We all have our own opinions as to what constitutes fortune. But Jesus proceeds to turn these ideas upside down.

The first lucky people he mentions are the "poor in spirit"; this would have shocked his listeners. Not the spiritual leaders. Not those who are confident in their ability to live righteous lives. No, it's the humble folk who are truly lucky—those who feel clumsy when it comes to spiritual matters. They are fortunate because God's kingdom belongs to them.

We could dig into that first Beatitude for quite a while, but let's zero in on the second instead. "Blessed are those who mourn." Not the smiley faces. Not those who bravely soldier on as if nothing happened. When people suffer a great loss, they need to mourn. They need to weep for weeks, if that's what it takes. They need to fall apart at the seams. They need to feel as if they can't go on. Jesus says people are lucky if they mourn.

**There is a comfort and a strength in love; 'Twill make a thing endurable, which else Would overset the brain, or break the heart.**

**—William Wordsworth, "A Pastoral Poem"**

Why? Modern psychology gives us one answer. When you hold back your true feelings, you do damage to yourself. Keeping a stiff upper lip sounds like a great plan, but it hurts you in the long run—both physically and emotionally. Our feelings were made to come out, and when we bottle them up, it puts great stress on our hearts, nerves, and immune system. Some people (especially men, but not exclusively) are taught from childhood to hold back emotions such as sorrow and grief. It can be therapeutic for such people to learn to let it out. Those who know how to mourn are the lucky ones.

But Jesus gives us a different answer. Mourners are blessed because "they will be comforted." There is something in the act of comforting that is good for us.

*Comfort, dear God, those whose eyes are filled with tears and those whose backs are near breaking with the weight of a heavy burden. Heal those whose hearts hold a wound and whose faith has been dealt a blow. Bless all who mourn and who despair. Help those who can't imagine how they'll make it through another day. For your goodness and mercy are enough for all the troubles in the world. Amen.*

I believe in some blending of hope and sunshine sweetening the worst lots. I believe that this life is not all; neither the beginning nor the end. I believe while I tremble; I trust while I sleep.

—Charlotte Brontë, *Villette*

*O Lord, hear my prayer for all who are in trouble this day. Comfort those who have lost a loved one. After the wrenching grief, let their hours be filled with fond memories of days gone by. Encourage those who find it difficult to believe in the future.*

*Bring wise friends into their lives who have long known the reality of your love. Let them be assured that you can take care of every need. Heal those who are suffering. Let them find rest and calm. Cradle their minds in your love and soothe every irrational thought that seeks to run out of control. May they find joy in just one moment at a time. And may that be enough for now.*

*In all these ways I ask your blessing upon those in trouble. And please include me in that blessing too!*

# New Connections

Perhaps there's someone who has stepped forward to help you in your time of grief. You now have a better, deeper relationship with this person. In some cases it's surprising who steps forward. Maybe someone you wouldn't expect has become an important friend in this time. Often it's someone who has recently experienced a loss and knows that pain firsthand. A new connection is created as these difficult emotions are shared.

"How very good and pleasant it is when kindred live together in unity!" sings a psalmist (Psalm 133:1). That sounds wonderful, but the truth is that our world can be quite isolating at times. Everyone fends for him or herself. People keep their deepest needs private. Sometimes it feels as if we live in little cubicles, never fully connecting with anyone. But the act of mourning and being comforted breaks down those barriers, as people reach out to help. As a result, we can all enjoy those "good and pleasant" relationships the psalmist is lauding.

But it's not just other people who comfort us when we mourn. We also receive comfort from God. Paul calls him "the God of all consolation, who consoles us in all our affliction" (2 Corinthians 1:3–4). We were just exploring the deeper relationships that come from the comfort we receive from other people. The same is certainly true with God. In our time of deepest sorrow, we fall into his arms. We are emptied of all our pretense. Any hint of phony religion or proud posturing is gone. We simply have nothing left. And God meets us there.

**The thread of our life would be dark, heaven knows, if it were not with friendship and love intertwined.**

**—Thomas More, *"Oh! Think Not My Spirits Are Always as Light"***

The act of mourning cuts through a lot of our normal game-playing with God. When we experience the devastating grief of a major loss, we are reduced to the level of need. We have no gift to bring to the altar this time. We just crawl before the Lord and cry.

He embraces us. He gives us the strength to put one foot in front of the other. He stirs our emotions so they can heal properly. He brings caring people around us. In the process, we learn to trust him more and more. Our relationship deepens.

That seems to be Jesus' main point in all these Beatitudes. The lucky ones are not the rich and proud but the poor and needy. Why? Because they have the amazing experience of relying on God for their daily sustenance, their future hope, and their ongoing comfort.

So don't feel bad for feeling bad. Jesus blessed your grief. You have enough to deal with right now without feeling guilty for grieving. You don't have to "cheer up." The sun may not come out tomorrow. In fact, your forecast is likely to be partly cloudy for several more months. Grieving takes time.

But even as you feel the deep sorrow of your loss, you can appreciate those friends who sit beside you and hold your hand. You can deepen friendships with those who weep with you. And you can slowly become aware that the God of consolation is wrapping you in his loving embrace.

The glory of God is evident in all his vast creation. The glory of God is in love, music, good food, and laughter. But the glory of God is also in pain and suffering—when people are called upon to be more of themselves and to help one another cope. It is in the darkest times that humankind becomes more like God: stronger, resilient, full of faith. It is easy to see God's glory in good things. The truly wise person sees the glory of God even in the bad.

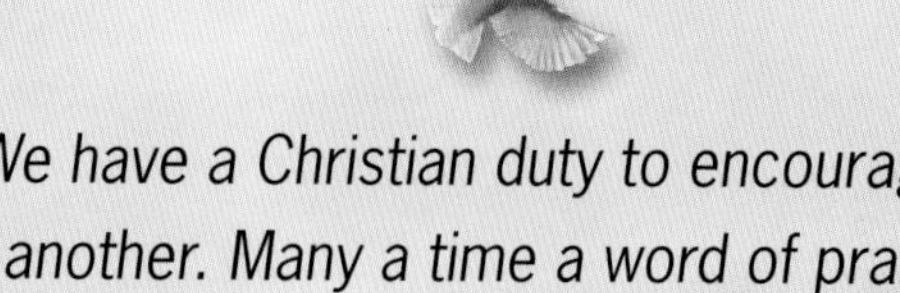

*We have a Christian duty to encourage one another. Many a time a word of praise or thanks or appreciation or cheer has kept a man on his feet. Blessed is the man who speaks such a word.*

—William Barclay, *The Gospel of Matthew*

*Think not thou canst sigh a sigh*
*And thy maker is not by;*
*Think not thou canst weep a tear*
*And thy maker is not near.*
*O! he gives to us his joy*
*That our grief he may destroy;*
*Till our grief is fled and gone*
*He doth sit by us and moan.*

—William Blake, "On Another's Sorrow"

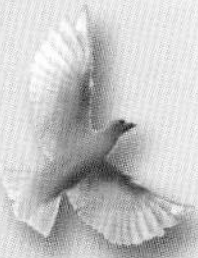

To receive the blessings of healing, the heart must be open. When we are grieving, it is so easy to close off the heart, sure that we will never be able to love again. But a heart that is shut down cannot receive understanding, acceptance, and renewal. Though we feel angry and afraid, we must keep the heart's door ajar so that God's grace can enter and fill our darkness with the light of hope.

# One More Thought

As you look around for comforters, you'll find the best ones among the weak, not among the strong. You don't need preachers with all the words or theologians with all the answers. You need someone who has been hurt as you've been hurt. You need people who understand you but probably think they don't. These are the people who will let you find your own way through grief but are willing to go there with you.

These have been called "wounded healers," and they follow in the footsteps of a Savior who saves us not because he's the Lord of Lords, but because he was wounded for us.

There's an amazing sentence early in Paul's second letter to the Corinthians. He praises "the God of all consolation"—and of the next 65 words, eight of them are the word "console/consolation." Basically, God consoles/comforts us so we can take that comfort and comfort others. (And Paul himself comforted and was comforted by the Corinthians, who comforted each other—you get the idea.) Apart from all the wordplay, the point is clear: The best comforters are those who have suffered and received comfort. That's the kind of person you want comforting you.

And we don't want to jump ahead too far, but there's a job for you down the road. When things start to turn around for you, and they will, you can begin reaching out to others—not with some sunny, cheery, otherworldly positivism, but with down-to-earth, nitty-gritty, real-world understanding. You already have the main qualification for the job of comforter: You have suffered. So file that away for future use. It might just provide some meaning for this whole painful experience.

*I thank my God every time I remember you, constantly praying with joy.*

—Philippians 1:3–4

God promises us his comfort, but he also uses us as his agents to comfort others. In fact, the difficulties we've gone through often give us the ability to reassure others who are now going through the same experiences. How will God use you to extend comfort to someone else?

*Bear one another's burdens, and in this way you will fulfill the law of Christ.*

—Galatians 6:2

Is there anything more painful than the death of a loved one—a precious parent, spouse, friend, child? When such a loss occurs, we feel the world should stop turning—all life should freeze in its tracks, just as time seems to have stopped for us. And yet, life goes on, despite our protests. And, impossible though it seems at first, healing can and does take place. With honest grieving, understanding friends, and the passage of time, it becomes possible to cope and begin living for ourselves again. After all, it does not dishonor the dead to take care of the living, even as we treasure our memories of our lost ones.

## *Chapter 11*

# Times of Discouragement

***Will life ever get back to normal? This grieving process might seem to take forever, but there is light at the end of the tunnel.***

*I believe that I shall see the goodness
of the Lord in the land of the living.
Wait for the Lord; be strong,
and let your heart take courage;
wait for the Lord!*

—Psalm 27:13–14

# Doing It Right?

It was a burden on Rachel when her father died. Her brother had been feuding with Dad and wanted nothing to do with him. Her mother was so distraught she couldn't do much. It was up to Rachel to communicate with the hospice staff in his final weeks, and it was up to her to tell her dad it was all right to let go. She had some rewarding talks with him in those final days, but she was taking time from her own husband and kids, and the stress was considerable.

Of course it was up to her to plan the funeral, and she did it well. "I can't even think about crying until all this is over," she told a friend. Indeed the responsibility was an emotional shield for her in the short term. She shed plenty of tears when she had the opportunity.

Some time later, she got wind of a bit of gossip that deeply bothered her. Some friend of the family was suggesting that Rachel must not have been on good terms with her father because she "seemed just fine" at the funeral. "She wasn't crying at all." When Rachel heard that, her anger was volcanic. She wanted to throw things. Her husband kept her from calling that woman and giving her a piece of her mind.

It was downright discouraging. Apparently, no one appreciated all she had done for the family. Her previously smooth recovery took a little detour.

So we do not lose heart. . . . our inner nature is being renewed day by day.

—2 Corinthians 4:16

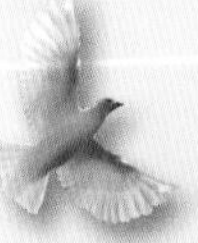

*God,*

*How long will this grief last? Shouldn't I feel better by now? People tell me to get on with my life, but I'm still full of sadness about my loss.*

*Please, God, help me understand my pain. Give my aching heart rest. Show me that your comfort is available to me.*

*Thank you for your love and assurance. Amen.*

*O let him whose sorrow*
*no relief can find,*
*Trust in God, and borrow*
*ease for the heart and mind.*
*Where the mourner weeping*
*sheds the secret tear,*
*God His watch is keeping,*
*though none else be near.*
*God will never leave thee,*
*All thy wants He knows,*
*Feels the pains that grieve thee,*
*sees thy cares and woes.*
*Raise thine eyes to Heaven*
*when thy spirits quail,*
*When, by tempests driven,*
*heart and courage fail.*
*All thy woe and sadness,*
*in this world below,*
*Balance not the gladness*
*thou in Heaven shalt know.*

—Heinrich Siegmund Oswald, "O Let Him Whose Sorrow"

# Stuff Happens

All sorts of things can discourage you when you're trying to get over your grief and get on with your life. You may have angry outbursts, which make you say, "Where did that come from?" There will be weepy nights and listless days. You will find vivid reminders of your loss in the most unexpected places, and they may take your breath away. Any of these things can puncture your balloon, convincing you that you'll never get back to anything close to normal. And *that's* discouraging.

***Renewed stress.*** Part of the recovery process involves a return to your normal expenditure of energy. In the throes of grief, you probably lightened your load a little. You begged out of social engagements, you stepped down from leadership roles, you shelved some personal projects. But as you've progressed in your grief recovery, you added some of these things back in. That can be tiring. Chances are, you're not quite functioning at 100-percent capacity just yet. You might be at 80 or 90 percent, but the additional stress of your normal schedule is too much for you. Your physical fatigue combines with emotional tenderness to create a sense of discouragement. Will you ever get up to speed?

> **He has made everything suitable for its time; moreover, he has put a sense of past and future into their minds.**
>
> **—Ecclesiastes 3:11**

What's more, your grief has taken a toll on your body. Crying puts your body through a physical workout, but *not* crying can have an even greater effect. People jam down their grief, physically, and that can result in a number of physical health issues. Even if you've been sitting at home doing very little, your body has been under stress. Your grief might have caused some sleepless nights or loss of appetite. It might have made you eat or drink or smoke more. It might have affected your sex life. It might have kept you from getting the exercise you need. It's as if

you've been training for a marathon, and *now* you add extra stressful activities. It's not surprising if you run out of steam sooner than you think you should. Still, it can be discouraging.

***Powerful memories.*** You will catch a whiff of some scent that reminds you of the one you've lost, and that will send you reeling. You will hear a voice that reminds you of that person's voice. You will hear a few notes of a song that you shared. A telephone ring tone, a color, a TV show, a spring day—anything can spark a sudden memory that will summon tears. This is not an indication that you're going backward in your recovery. Accept it as a gift.

Karen lost a dear friend 25 years ago, just out of college. It was a devastating loss at the time. The friend she lost, Leigh, was an unusually insightful young woman, brilliantly creative and deeply spiritual. Karen felt the world was impoverished when a rare cancer claimed Leigh's life, and she grieved heavily for a couple of years. That was long ago, but recently Karen caught a glimpse of a woman who reminded her of Leigh. Rather, it was an image of what Leigh might have looked like had she lived to middle age. Seeing this woman struck Karen to the core, and she began to grieve again for the loss of this irreplaceable woman. As it happens, Karen is currently tending to two other irreplaceable women with terminal illnesses—her mother and her best friend—so she is certainly in grieving mode. But the memory of Leigh did not send her reeling; it made her thankful for the time she'd had with that extraordinary woman . . . and the other extraordinary women in her life.

***Ignorant people.*** The world never seems to run out of them. As Rachel discovered, people are quick to pry and make pronouncements on things they know nothing about. Are you grieving enough? Are you grieving too much? Shouldn't you be over this by now? (That's what they're saying.) Some of these folks might prey upon your familial obligations. Isn't it damaging to the children to show grief so openly?

Of course there's always the faith component, and we've already discussed that a bit. True faith helps a great deal in your grieving, but faith doesn't help much when it's hypocritical, pious, or shallow. People might start questioning your Christian credentials—at exactly the time when you're encountering some serious doubts yourself. Stadiums could be filled with people who have left their churches in these situations—not because they're angry with God (though that is often an issue), but because they're upset with the Christians who aren't letting them grieve as they need to.

Psalms 42 and 43 provide an interesting study in discouragement and hope. "As a deer longs for flowing streams," the psalmist begins, "so my soul longs for you, O God." He talks about his thirst for God, his desire to encounter God face to face. He's weeping constantly, but people are asking, "Where is your God?" At first glance this seems like atheists taunting him, ridiculing his faith. But what if it's the issue we've discussed here—people of faith questioning *your* faith, as if your overwhelming tears are evidence of the fact that you've lost touch with God.

This idea may be borne out in Psalm 42:4: "These things I remember, as I pour out my soul: how I went with the throng, and led them in procession to the house of God, with glad shouts and songs of thanksgiving." This man used to be a worship leader, but now his soul is "cast down . . . disquieted." Has he been ostracized from the community? Are people judging him?

The psalmist returns, again and again, to a simple statement of faith—no complex theology here, just a cry of the heart—"Hope in God; for I shall again praise him, my help and my God."

Ignorant people can be damaging. Ignorant *religious* people can be even worse. Brush them off, and keep to your course. Some things are between you and God.

*Creator God,*

*I know you created me, all of me. You made my laughter, but also my tears. You crafted the processes of my heart and mind. You know when I need to come face-to-face with reality, and you know when I can only deal with it in small doses. You understand me better than I do.*

*The truth is, I'm confused sometimes by my own behavior. I try to be positive, but then I'm crying my eyes out. I try to have a good cry, and I end up irritated over silly things. I try to vent my anger, and I feel guilty about that. And then I feel guilty for feeling guilty.*

*This is a difficult road I'm on, Lord. I ask that you travel it with me. Hold me close. I'm not asking you to cheer me up all the time, just let me know that you're beside me, behind me, guiding me along. I don't need to know that today I'm a step beyond where I was yesterday. Can you go with me step by step?*

*Thank you, my loving Lord. Amen.*

*My Creator, I know in my heart that these tears will one day give way again to joy, yet for now I know only pain. Help me find the courage to let these tears flow, to feel the loss and heartbreak, so that I may come out whole and cleansed again. For on the other side of my sorrow I know life waits for me. I want to laugh again.*

# Reorganization

Experts have analyzed and reanalyzed the grief process. One now-classic way of understanding it is the five stages of grief, which we've talked about in this book. That system was developed a few decades ago and still provides a broad framework. But of course many psychology students with a doctoral thesis to write want to improve on that, and a number of other systems have been offered, some of these quite helpful. One system focuses on certain "tasks" of the grieving process, and we've used some of that language here as well. You may have special kinds of work to do in each of these "times" you go through—grieving, remembering, protesting, integrating, etc.

The words vary from system to system, but the effect is generally the same. Grief recovery means coming to an acceptance of what has happened and reconfiguring your life in such a way that you can go on without the one you've lost. It's almost a binary system in play here, with competing Yes and No statements.

*No, I don't believe this happened.*
*Yes, it happened.*
*No, it's not right that it happened.*
*Yes, I'll accept it and move on.*
*No, I can't bear this sadness.*
*Yes, I must find a way.*

And so on. That's what makes this such an interesting process to analyze—there are many variations on Yes and No. That also makes it a difficult process to go through. For every three steps forward, it seems there are two steps back.

*Yes, I think I've finally recovered.*
*No, not so fast.*

One newer system presents the stages of grief as Protest, Searching, Despair, Reorganization, and Reinvestment. We've already looked at several elements of those first three stages. That's where you find denial, anger, and deep sadness.

But discouragement is common in the Reorganization stage. One approach (by Bess Bailey and Peter Lynch) lists these symptoms of Reorganization:

- Bursts of energy
- Intermittent interest
- Indifference
- Fatigue
- Detachment
- Apathy

Those are not qualities you'd want to see in someone you hire to remodel your home, much less in reorganizing your life. Yet the truth is that you're weary from the long process of Protest, Searching, and Despair. You're trying to put some kind of life back together, and there are bursts of energy when you're actually succeeding... and then something happens to discourage you. What's the use?

**Let us therefore approach the throne of grace with boldness, so that we may receive mercy and find grace to help in the time of need.**

**—Hebrews 4:16**

In *About Mourning,* Savine Gross Weizman and Phyllis Kamm discuss the ups and downs of the grieving process: "Mourners are extremely sensitive and a fleeting thought, a small incident, or a word from someone else can cause a sudden mood change. It is surprising how quickly you can go from up to down.... When you feel better, you may think, 'Everything is going to be all right from now on. I am going to be able to go on with my life.' However, before long there is another mood swing into sadness again. Many people are discouraged by this.... There are periods of hopefulness and periods of hopelessness. Over a period of time the mood changes lessen and the periods of sadness shorten."

All adventure movies have a series of ups and downs as the protagonists pursue their goal, whatever that might be. If there were only ups, it wouldn't be a very interesting movie, would it? In most of them, there's an extremely discouraging moment about 20 minutes from the end of the movie. You thought they were going to reach their goal, it was within their grasp, but no, something happens to make it impossible. You wonder how there will ever be a happy ending. But of

course, thanks to movie magic, heroes overcome impossible odds to win the day.

Maybe you have fought through the protest and searching, the denial and anger. Maybe you have waded through despair and the deep sadness of your loss. Maybe you are trying to reorganize your life in a way that will, no, never lead you to forget the one you've lost but, yes, move you forward toward a better life. And maybe some little comment, some event, some strain of an old song has knocked you for a loop. If so, then you're at the 20-minute mark. You might be discouraged for the moment, but buck up, there's a happy ending ahead.

*Why are you cast down, O my soul,*
*and why are you disquieted within me?*
*Hope in God; for I shall again praise him,*
*my help and my God.*

—Psalm 42:11

*Lord of second chances,*

*Just when I thought I had this handled, I slipped back. I was feeling almost healthy again. I actually cracked a smile, I think. After months of heartache, that's really something. For a moment I envisioned a future—yes, a future without the one I've lost, but a future full of precious memories. It was there, in front of me, almost within reach... and then I got upset again, and the tears were flowing, and I was saying and thinking things I didn't want to say or think. I'm not sure what happened.*

*Lord, I ask you to cover me with your love. Let your Spirit fill my heart. Whisper your assurances to me every day. Give me another chance to put my heart back together. Calm the hurricane that rages inside me.*

*And please be patient with me. I'm likely to stir up a new storm as soon as you've soothed the old one. These days I'm celebrating every step forward by taking two steps back. I need your power in my life, pulling me forward. Restore the joy of my salvation.*

*I ask this humbly. Amen.*

When drooping pleasure turns to grief,
And trembling faith is changed to fear,
The murmuring wind, the quivering leaf,
Shall softly tell us, Thou are near!

—Oliver Wendell Holmes, "Hymn of Trust"

# What You Can Do

Are there ways you can keep discouragement from derailing you? Here are some things you could consider.

***Guard your physical health.*** You know the drill: Eat right, exercise, get plenty of sleep, take vitamins, cut back on the smoking, drinking, and sweets. This might not be easy to do all at once, especially if you're out of the habit. But make a list, schedule it out, and get started on a physical health plan.

Keep your short-term goals small and reasonable, and build from there. (You don't need another kind of discouragement from failing to reach overambitious physical goals.) Don't focus on results (like losing a certain number of pounds) but on the process (like working out once or twice a week).

***Muster support.*** We noted earlier that your supportive group might dwindle over time. At the funeral, they're saying, "Whatever you need, call me." But they forget about you after three months. (They're not bad people, just busy.) It's up to you to gather your support team. Explain to them that you're still dealing with your loss and you need them to check up on you in certain ways. "I'm doing better than I was, but I still have a ways to go. Could you help keep me on track?" They can listen to you, encourage you, and gently nudge you forward when you need it.

***Mark the holidays.*** Hospice care often provides follow-up for families for 13 months after the death of their loved one. Why that period? They know that even if you think you're all better after one year, the anniversary may knock you back down. You can anticipate setbacks on birthdays, holidays, and any other dates that were significant to you and the deceased. Do not be discouraged if on these days you revert back to anger or depression. It's pretty normal. You'll get back up and resume the healing process.

***Mete out your stress.*** Be careful how much stress you take on in your work, family, community, or church activities. Say no when you need to. You don't always have to give a reason, but you could say, "I'm still dealing with the death of this loved one, and it's probably wise not to push myself too much too soon." Over the next few years you'll probably get back to your preloss levels of activity, but right now you're still on "injured reserve." Take it as slow as you need to.

***Set yourself a task.*** Outside stressors should be carefully regulated, but it might be good to push yourself slightly. (This is especially true for men, who tend to heal through activity rather than conversation.) Is there some sort of project you could take on—perhaps something that you can dedicate to the loved one you've lost? Some have planted gardens, done some woodworking, or composed songs. Sometimes the long period of grief recovery can feel like a waste, but this is something tangible you can accomplish. Don't push yourself too hard—you don't need extra stress—but let this be a labor of love that you can offer as a memorial and also as a way to reclaim yourself.

I awoke at dawn one morning
From a restless night of sorrow,
Praying that with the daylight
Might come a bright tomorrow.
My heart as cold and hopeless
At winter's deepest chill,
I cried out for understanding
And to know my Father's will.
While treading up a garden path
Hushed in the fragrant air;
I spied a tender rose,
Its petals bowed as if in prayer.
As I gazed in silent awe,
It occurred to me—he knows!
The tears my Lord has shed for me
Are the dew upon the rose.

Chapter 12

# Times of Growth

***Every hard time builds us up, even when we think we're being torn down. Maybe you're reaching a point where you're ready to see the ways you have grown stronger.***

Very truly, I tell you, unless a grain of wheat falls into the earth and dies, it remains just a single grain; but if it dies, it bears much fruit.

—John 12:24

# Finding Out Who You Are

Mitch was a "mistake," and growing up he often felt like one. Without getting into all the details, his father and mother had both been married to other people and had children with those spouses. Mitch's conception was actually the crisis that brought about his parent's wedding. You might say he was the runt of the litter, with lots of older brothers and sisters, some much older, from those previous marriages.

His dad never had much time for him, and so he grew up rather independently. A sweet, caring guy, Mitch connected with a great group of friends. That's how he developed an interest in the arts, something his dad cared little about.

He wasn't rebellious or hateful, just sort of mystified by this stranger who had sired him. As an adult, Mitch would see his parents at least once a week, but there wasn't much to talk about. His artistic life was foreign to them, and their history seemed shrouded in secrecy. Occasionally he would watch a football game with his dad, and that was good. They were both avid fans.

**Trouble and anguish have come upon me, but your commandments are my delight. . . . give me understanding that I may live.**

**—Psalm 119:143–144**

Things changed a bit when Mitch got married and had kids. His folks were great babysitters, and this gave them even more opportunity to connect. But while the children were still rather young, Mitch's dad was diagnosed with several serious health problems. As these grew worse, it became apparent that he would die soon. Mitch was there often in the final weeks, and he would hear family stories that amazed him—his dad's exploits, problems with the extended family, and some of the emotional background surrounding his own birth and upbringing. Some of the stories were shocking, but Mitch was more surprised that it had taken 35 years for him to hear them. In some ways, he felt he was finally being welcomed into the family.

Then his father died, and the funeral was strange. Some of the siblings took the opportunity to make the event far more religious than their father actually was. With the whole family around, Mitch was generally overlooked.

Afterward, the siblings began bickering over the distribution of their father's things. But somehow Mitch had been named executor, and it fell to him to restore order—which he did with a wisdom that surprised even him.

"I miss him," Mitch says now. "It's just strange that he's not there." Mitch doesn't really feel anger, though you would easily excuse him if he did. And he doesn't feel regret, as if he should have done things differently. He just feels a kind of emptiness.

There's also a greater awareness of his own mortality. His dad was four decades ahead of him, so it's not like Mitch is ready to pack it in, but a generation has advanced. Mitch is not a little kid anymore; he's now a patriarch.

For Mitch and for many others, grieving the death of a loved one means gaining a whole new understanding of themselves. There is growth to be found in these difficult times. We miss those we've lost, and we can weep and mope and shake our fists at the heavens, but through it all we emerge stronger, more resilient, more in touch with what really matters.

# No Ordinary Joe

The Old Testament character of Joseph gives us a great example of growth through struggle. When we first meet him, he's a brash young man, the apple of his father's eye. He parades around in the fine coat his father gave him, and he eagerly tells his brothers about his dreams, in which they generally end up bowing down to him. His brothers go out to the fields to tend the family flocks while Joseph stays home in comfort. You can imagine how the brothers feel about him.

When Dad sends him out to check on them, they hatch their plot, selling Joseph into slavery and telling their dad he's dead. Finally they're rid of the annoying dreamer.

At this point, Joseph would be starting a grief recovery process. He is mourning a death: his own. His father thinks he's dead, and he might as well be. He has lost everything—his comfort, his status, his relationships. The Bible doesn't give us all the details of his grief, but the next stages of the story take several years. We might guess that he took a while to deal with denial and anger before he decided to try to be the best slave he could be.

And so we see Joseph making the best of a bad situation, until it gets worse. His master's wife falsely accuses him of rape, and he's thrown into prison. Again we might expect some sort of grief process to begin anew. But eventually he reconstructs his life. He revises his dreams. He realizes he will never be a rancher in Canaan like his dad. He'll just have to be the best prisoner he can be.

He earns the warden's trust, and he makes friends with a couple of outcasts from the royal court, and eventually, after two more years of wallowing in confinement, Joseph gets a break. Pharaoh's butler, now restored to royal service, remembers that Joseph had a knack for interpreting dreams. Joseph is called before the pharaoh to do his thing.

It's his one opportunity to hit the big time, and he doesn't miss. The dream predicts good times and then bad times. The secret to success, Joseph says, is to save up in the good times so you'll have enough for the bad. We might wonder whether that was a lesson he wished he had learned earlier. Back in his own good times, should he have learned better people skills? Should he have "saved up" good will with his brothers?

In any event, Joseph suggests that he could be pharaoh's special economic assistant, and pharaoh agrees. The kid from Canaan is back on top now. His recovery is over...or is it? His father still thinks he's dead, and his brothers probably assume he has died in oblivion.

The next act of this script is the family reunion. Jacob sends his sons to Egypt to get food in this terrible time of famine. Joseph plays some games with them, making sure their hearts have softened. Ultimately he reveals himself, tearfully, and his father is brought to Egypt to join them.

Happy ending. Well, almost. Some years later, after the whole family has settled in Egypt, the father dies, and the brothers worry that Joseph will now take his revenge on them. Perhaps he has carried a grudge all these years and was just holding back for Dad's sake. After all, he's a high-ranking Egyptian official now. He could have them squashed like bugs.

But Joseph makes a tremendous comment that indicates how much he has grown in all these years. "Even though you intended to do harm to me," he says, "God intended it for good" (Genesis 50:20).

Wrap your mind around that for a moment. *This was an evil thing you guys did, but God did a good thing through it.* We can apply that to every misfortune Joseph faced. His master's wife was vicious, selfish, and deceitful when she falsely accused Joseph—she intended evil, but God intended good. Pharaoh's butler was negligent when he waited two years to put in a good word for Joseph. His oversight could have done more harm to Joseph, but God turned it to good.

So let's talk about you. The loss you have faced is a bad thing. There's no question about that. Don't let anyone suggest that the pain isn't real. It is a tragic event. You can talk all you want about silver linings and all things working together. That doesn't change the fact that this hurts. You have lost someone you dearly love.

But that's not the final word. According to Joseph, even intentional harm can be turned to good. As God works his healing, kneading it through every situation of our lives, some good things can happen *even in the midst of the bad things.*

One of the good things that can happen is your growth. Do you come out of this painful time stronger, more focused? Do you have a clearer sense of what's most important in life? Do you treasure relationships more? Are you more motivated to do something better with your own life?

**And the one who was seated on the throne said, "See, I am making all things new. . . . To the thirsty I will give water as a gift from the spring of the water of life."**

**—Revelation 21:5–6**

An observation about personal growth: We generally don't recognize when it's happening. It often feels like something else—hardship, challenge, opportunity. But only looking back do we see what has happened. We notice that we're doing things differently, that we're thinking or feeling at a different level than we were before. Only later do we see how much we've grown.

Going through a difficult time alone feels like trying to find your way through a pitch-black room. The moment you reach out to another, a light appears that guides you to the other side, where the door to healing awaits. Faith in a wise and trustworthy God, even in grievous times like these, teaches us a new math: subtracting old ways and adding new thoughts because sharing with God divides our troubles and sadness and multiplies unfathomable possibilities for renewed life. After you bow your head in mourning, lift your head in faith.

*A new heart I will give you, and a new spirit I will put within you; and I will remove from your body the heart of stone and give you a heart of flesh.*

—Ezekiel 36:26

Weeping may linger for the night,
but joy comes with the morning.

—Psalm 30:5

*My Redeemer,*

*I don't know how you're going to do it. I feel like such a wreck right now, like I have nothing to offer. This ordeal has sapped me. It has driven me down into the dirt, and it has made me feel things I never want to feel again. But you want to turn all of that into something positive? I can't imagine what that would be, but I'm willing to let you try.*

*Take my life, and let it be something beautiful for thee. Amen.*

# The Challenge

It should have been a time of great celebration. Instead it was full of concern. Brian and Darlene were expecting their first child, but the delivery was difficult, and the child was in serious condition. The doctors managed to keep the baby alive for a few weeks. Those were agonizing weeks for the young parents, days and nights in the hospital, hoping against hope, yet fearing the worst.

They were not very religious people. They attended church occasionally, but they both had professional careers. Who had time? But now their lives caved in as they watched the struggles of their newborn son, Jeremy. Prayers were flying heavenward, but would God really listen to a couple of part-time Christians?

Folks at their church got wind of the situation and rallied to support them. Suddenly, people

Brian and Darlene hardly knew were bringing them meals, sending them cards of encouragement, and offering to sit with them at the hospital. And, above all, they prayed for the young family.

Finally little Jeremy lost his struggle. His parents were devastated, but the church members stepped up their support. Over the next year, as Brian and Darlene worked through the grieving process, they were impressed by the caring nature of these Christians. The experience had shown these two affluent professionals how impoverished they were spiritually. They simply had no resources to get them through that crisis. Yet that was exactly what the church members had—and freely shared. The grieving parents, each in their own way, had a kind of conversion. The faith they had followed casually now became important in their lives. They got involved in the church and began serving others, just as they had been served.

Looking back, they say it was their son Jeremy who brought them to Jesus.

You might not want to hear this right now, but it's true. Your greatest triumph may come from your worst calamity. Brian and Darlene are not alone. For many people, the tragedy of losing a loved one forces them to ask important questions—eternal questions. Coming so close to death makes us consider how precious life is. And what are we doing with that precious gift? Some find that bereavement propels them into action, as they try to make the most of whatever time they have left.

We think that our pain is weakening us. We expect that our doubts will damage our faith. We assume that our future will be bleaker. But the truth is usually different. The crises we face tend to make us stronger. Through the sorrow, we develop character, wisdom, and strength.

In the Old Testament, God talks about "refining" his people like silver. "I have tested you in the furnace of adversity" (Isaiah 48:10). In the refining process, the impurities are burned out of metal, making the metal that much stronger.

The New Testament picks up on that idea in several places. "My brothers and sisters," writes James, "whenever you face trials of any kind, consider it nothing but joy, because you know that the testing of your faith produces endurance; and let endurance have its full effect, so that you may be mature and complete, lacking in nothing" (James 1:2–4). Paul talks about boasting in his sufferings, "knowing that suffering produces endurance, and endurance produces character, and character produces hope, and hope does not disappoint us, because God's love has been poured into our hearts" (Romans 5:3–5).

You might feel that your grief will overwhelm you, that it will never go away. But, in fact, it is helping you grow. You will emerge from this a better person. As Psalm 30 tells us, the Lord can turn mourning into dancing. You can't ignore the sadness of losing your loved one, but you can eventually grow into a celebration of that person's life—and your own.

# Using the Down Time

How can you use your time of grieving to grow stronger? Consider these possibilities:

***Experience God in a new way.*** Try being radically honest with him. Or try picturing the Lord weeping beside you. Count on him for strength as you deal with your grief. Brian and Darlene were jolted into a new relationship with God. Maybe that can happen for you.

***Exercise your emotions.*** Maybe you are already a very emotional person, but if you're not, this time of grieving can help you reconnect with your feelings. Our society today tends to discourage open displays of emotion. As a result, many people bottle themselves up. Our strong reactions to the passing of a loved one can free us up to feel in ways that have long been dormant.

***Excavate your issues.*** This might be an opportunity to evaluate the way you relate to others. Consider your relationship with the loved one you've lost. It probably had some good aspects and some bad ones. You might harbor regrets or grudges. It might be healthy to get these out in the open. Proceed with care here, because your feelings might be pretty raw. You might want to work with a pastor or counselor on this, but if it's done well, it could teach you a lot about yourself as you move forward.

Healing is a matter of time, but it is sometimes a matter of opportunity.

—Hippocrates

***Express compassion to others.*** In the future, when you meet anyone else who is grieving, you can say, "I've been there. I understand what you're feeling." You know what it's like, and that empowers you to sit beside others and offer help. It is an exhilarating feeling to "pay forward" the comfort you have received from others. When you use your own difficult experiences to enable you to comfort someone else, that's a powerful piece of redemption.

*How often we look upon God as our last and feeblest resource? We go to him because we have nowhere else to go. And then we learn that the storms of life have driven us, not upon the rocks, but into the desired haven.*

—George MacDonald

*He that lacks time to mourn,*
*lacks time to mend.*
*Eternity mourns that.*
*'Tis an ill cure for life's worst ills,*
*to have no time to feel them.*
*Where sorrow's held intrusive*
*and turned out,*
*There wisdom will not enter, nor true power,*
*Nor aught that dignifies humanity.*

—Sir Henry Taylor

It takes moral courage to grieve.
It requires religious courage to rejoice.

—Søren Kierkegaard

*Like a toddler who falls more than he stands, I'm pulling myself upright in the aftermath of death. I know you as a companion, God of mending hearts, and feel you steadying me. Thank you for the gift of resilience. Lead me to others who have hurt and gone on; I need to see how it's done.*

Happiness is beneficial to the body, but it is grief that develops the powers of the mind.

—Marcel Proust

Chapter 13

# Times of Remembrance

***From time to time, memories of your loved one will come back to you—causing both tears and laughter. What can you do with these memories? Are they helpful or hurtful?***

*I thank my God every time I remember you.*

—Philippians 1:3

# Missing a Matriarch

They were a devout Christian family at the funeral of their 102-year-old matriarch. As they rode in the procession toward the cemetery, their conversation was upbeat. This was more of a beginning than an end. It was a graduation for this woman, who loved her Lord and looked forward to life in heaven. One family member after another commented on the joy of the occasion. She had lived a long, lovely life. This funeral was a celebration. Then the youngest granddaughter piped up. "Yeah, but I'm sad! I'm really going to miss her."

The positive approach of this family was perfectly legitimate. Everything they said was true. After more than a century, it's hard to begrudge a saint's trip to heaven. But all their theologizing was covering up the simple emotional fact that death is also sad. It separates us from our loved ones. Even when we're happy for them, it's natural to miss them terribly. We can be glad and sad at the same time.

*Dear God,*

*I'm going to start singing again. My voice has been quiet too long. Not that I'm "getting over" my grief. No, I doubt I'll ever recover entirely from the loss of this special person in my life. How can I? But I can sing again because this dear one would want me to. Because they are so important, I can celebrate every memory. I can live my life fully.*

*Celebrate with me, dear Lord. Amen.*

# Heartwarming Surprise

As you deal with your own grief, you might find some uplift for your spirit by remembering the life of your departed loved one and thanking God for it. Sometimes funerals or memorial services provide opportunities for various people to comment on what the deceased meant to them. It can be a heartwarming surprise to see how many people were touched by the life of the departed.

Pleasant but quiet, Gus worked for many years in the mailroom of a Christian ministry. The executives at that company viewed him as a sort of lovable loser. He wasn't very well educated, had few social skills, and suffered from an assortment of health problems—but he managed to do his job faithfully.

Gus passed away in his mid-40s, an untimely death but not surprising given his health history. Some of the staff of the ministry where he worked went to the funeral at a nearby church, and they were surprised by what they found. Since Gus was single and lived by himself, they expected only a smattering of relatives and friends, but the place was packed. Over the course of two hours, one person after another stood up and told of the kindness Gus had shown them. *He taught me to read. He drove me to church each Sunday. He helped me quit drinking. He got me a job.* The staff members were shocked; they had no idea what a great guy they'd been working with.

**How sweet the silent backward tracings! The wanderings as in dreams—the meditation of old times resumed—their loves, joys, person, voyages.**

**—Walt Whitman, "Memories"**

These public remembrances help us celebrate the life of someone we've lost. They give us perspective on the person's life. They provide us with a sense of thankfulness that can soften our grief. They also help us to say good-bye.

Of course we can find private ways to remember our departed loved ones as well. We can place pictures of them and various artifacts from their lives around our homes. Or you might choose to create photo albums to commemorate the person's life. Perhaps you could even put together a video or audio recording of various people's memories. Some folks might do something special in their loved one's honor—plant a tree, walk in the woods, skip stones on the river, walk barefoot in the rain, climb a mountain, ride a train, or do some other particular thing the departed loved. In those cases, it can feel as if the lost loved one is enjoying the activity too.

## A Memory Prayer

***Rewound and shown again, like old home movies, tales are being told, O Lord, by those of us facing this loss.***

***"Remember when?" we say laughing, interrupting one another in the retelling of time shared.***

*"Remember when?" We savor a final showing, reel upon reel, of pranks pulled, triumphs achieved, kindnesses shown, conversations held. "Remember when?"*

*We are grateful that you bring a last frame into focus for us, of life forever after, of rooms prepared for us. And while we shrink against daily life without this loved one, we're comforted knowing they've just gone on ahead.*

*Thank you, Lord, for adding the gift of memory to our days ahead, of helping us to "remember when."*

*Polish our memories of loved ones laid to rest here, Lord, and then strengthen our resolve for going on without them.*

# The Trouble with Remembrance

Some people have trouble with remembrances of their loved one. The grief might be too fresh. Especially in the early months of bereavement, being surrounded by reminders of the person might create unbearable sadness. Be sensitive to your own needs (and the needs of anyone else in your home). There are times when you want to remember and times when you don't.

What happens when the person you're commemorating wasn't such a saint? How can you memorialize someone you blame for messing up your life in one way or another? Do you grit your teeth and pretend they were perfect?

This is a problem for many who grieve the loss of their parents. They truly love and miss their folks, but there are all sorts of issues too.

Can you forgive someone after they're gone? Or should you just forget all the bad stuff?

Honesty is the best policy, but grace makes it even better. When we live in grace, we understand that we are sinners forgiven by God, and other people are too. We don't need to ignore the bad things done by those we've lost, but we shouldn't dwell on those things either. In cases where we've been wronged, we can offer forgiveness belatedly. Why not assume that the

person is straightening things out with the Lord right now and would be asking your forgiveness if that were possible? Would you grant that forgiveness?

In other cases, we find our memories haunted by our own sense of guilt and regret. We feel bad about things we did to the person who is now gone. For some reason, we never got around to seeking forgiveness, and now that is impossible.

**My friend lives on in me, in thought and memory, remembrance of the time we spent together. And though my friend is gone, our relationship goes on, for I know that friendship lasts forever.**

Or is it? That's a transaction you can bring before the Lord. Confess your sins and ask for God's forgiveness for whatever you did or didn't do with regard to your departed loved one. Ask him to clear the guilt from your memory.

Then you need to show grace to yourself. You're not perfect; that's a given. You could have done more, said more, loved more. Maybe your relationship with this person was not all it could have been. But you can still be thankful for what it was.

"I thank my God every time I remember you," the apostle Paul said (in some form) in nearly every epistle (see Ephesians 1:16; Philippians 1:3; 1 Thessalonians 1:2). And what memories did he have? Oh, he'd been arrested in some of these towns, beaten up, and jailed. In some of these churches, rival preachers came along with their trash talk, saying that Paul's teaching was bogus and they had a better way. Some congregations had bitter infighting. They weren't perfect, but Paul thanked God for them anyway.

And that's the attitude we can adopt toward our lost loved one—thankful remembrance—even though they weren't perfect and neither are we.

*Remember the days of old,*
*consider the years long past.*

—Deuteronomy 32:7

*Lord, it's the little things that mean the most. The tilt of the head. The corner of a smile. The hand on my hand, telling me it will be all right. Inhaling a cup of coffee. Gazing with awe at a stunning sunset. Holding a squirming baby and rocking it to sleep. These are the things I remember, and I miss them all, but I treasure each one.*

*Thank you for this life. Amen.*

It's a pleasure to share one's memories.
Everything remembered is dear, endearing,
touching, precious. At least the past is safe—
though we didn't know it at the time.
We know it now. Because it's in the past;
because we have survived.

—Susan Sontag

*My God,*

*Thank you for the life of the loved one I've lost. Yes, I've been grieving, and even scolding you a bit, but now I'm looking from a different angle. This dear one meant so much to me. You ministered to me through this person, and I am grateful. So instead of regretting the moments we'll no longer have together, I will savor the moments we had. Thank you. Amen.*

*I grieve what is lost forever. And yet words once heard float like mind-perfume, opening up a floodgate of memory, recalling the moments when those words were spoken. And I am comforted. Thank you, O God, for the gift of remembering.*

# Things of Remembrance Past

Dawn's father passed away in a nursing home, and before the family knew it, the room was cleaned up, his things packed up, the place locked up. She wanted to linger on some final sensations—the smell of his shirt, the texture of his blanket—but this was not possible. Her mother died at home, and after the funeral Dawn and her two sisters sat on Mom's bed crying and laughing and remembering, surrounded by all her stuff. There was something good and right about that.

You can't take it with you, they say, referring to the material accumulations of our lives. A person moves on to an eternal reward while leaving behind the things that he or she owned and used and treasured. Some of those items practically became part of them—his pipe, her glasses, his record collection, her china, the slippers he wore until noon each Saturday, the afghan she pulled around her to watch her favorite TV shows. These objects still carry their scent, their DNA, maybe even their personality. For those who loved these people, these things will always be vivid reminders.

Tammy has a ring her mother used to wear. Whenever she puts it on, she feels especially close to her mom, who passed away a few years ago. For this reason, she has designated certain pieces of her jewelry to go to her three kids, so they'll always have a connection with her.

Some might argue that this is silly. You don't need some trinket to remember a person, and that may indeed be true. But we are sensory people, and our memories fade over time. Our connections with these things aren't just mental, but tactile and visual and aural. We don't have to focus our minds on the memory of our departed loved ones; we can touch the memory, hold the memory, wear the memory. It makes perfect sense to treasure the items that they invested their lives in, because we can share some of that investment. We can feel some residue of their presence.

Not only do things remind us of our loved ones, they sort of *locate* our memories. Tombstones have long been used in this way. A person might head out to the cemetery, saying, "I'm going to go talk with mom." And they will stand in front of the tombstone, marking the place where Mom's body lies, and talk. As we've already said, such conversations can be therapeutic. Nothing is wrong with putting your feelings into words and launching them toward the spirit or memory of your lost loved one. What's interesting here is the spatial element. A person goes *to* the graveyard to hold this conversation. Is this necessary? Of course not. The conversation would be therapeutic wherever it's held. But there is something powerful in the person's commitment to go to that place. This isn't just a random thought tossed into the ether. It's a directed conversation.

The same sort of spatial power might occur with all sorts of objects that we associate with

the ones we've lost. We treat those items as if the spirit of our loved one resides in them. This can get a little spooky, but it can also be somewhat freeing. If I locate my memories of the person at that cemetery or in that room or in that stuffed animal, then I don't have to connect with those memories in other places. This is a very important factor as we move along in our recovery. We certainly don't want to lose those memories, but we do want to "put them in their place" (perhaps literally), so they're not constantly haunting us. That's why people might go to the gravesite to talk with Mom—because they don't want the pressure of holding those conversations in other times and places. It sort of cordons off that aspect of recovery.

The power of objects also works in the other direction. Not only do we receive memories of our loved ones through the things in their lives, we can also give honor to them with things we create. In her candid book *When Will I Stop Hurting?*, June Cerza Kolf tells of one woman who used her quilt-making ability to help in her healing. "The mother of a teenaged girl who was killed in a car accident sorted through her fabric remnants, took swatches of fabric from all the garments she had sewn for her daughter over the years, and made a quilt from them. She called it her 'loving memories' quilt. . . . The mother would handle the quilt in times of sorrow and feel her spirits lift."

You might use your own creativity to make a fitting memorial for your loved one. Can you paint a mural, plant a tree, build a nightstand, or make a video as a tribute to the one you've lost? Perhaps you can incorporate items from their life, as the quilt did, but this isn't necessary. And don't get too hung up on perfection here. This is your gift to your memory of this person. You want to pour yourself into it. Sure, you want it to be as good as it can be, but it's still *your* gift, and so rough edges and bold flourishes and unfinished corners might be very appropriate. Make it more personal than professional.

So you have pain now; but I will see you again, and your hearts will rejoice, and no one will take your joy from you.

—John 16:22

# Images and Actions

One man was grieving a son who died from injuries sustained in a playground accident. He used his organizational business skills to start a nonprofit foundation to build safer playgrounds. He poured his grief into this activity. In the extreme, this might prove to be a distraction from the grieving process, a way of avoiding emotion. But for many people, this is exactly how they express their emotions—by doing something.

Another man wrote a play about the wife he had recently lost, detailing their courtship and marriage. He presented it to a local theater director with hopes that it might be produced. Dramatically speaking, the play wasn't very good, but the director was gentle. He realized exactly what this was: an expression of grief and memory. He sweetly explained that, while he appreciated the passion and honesty of the piece, they would not be putting it on.

This points up a danger in these memorial actions. Will you be crushed if no one else appreciates them as you do? What if the playground foundation fell flat? What if the director had been critical of this heartfelt-but-amateurish play? Would that response have sent the person reeling? These concerns shouldn't keep you from attempting actions or creating objects to honor your loved one. Just be aware that this thing means more to you than to anyone else.

Images are extremely important to us as we try to hold on to memories of our loved ones. You may already have scads of pictures and videos you've taken over the years. Keep these. Cherish them. And go through them from time to time. If you don't have a picture collection, don't be shy about asking friends and family for copies of their pictures of the loved one you've lost. There is nothing wrong with wanting these images, and they'll probably be eager to help.

If you have any recordings of the person's voice, even a voicemail message, preserve them.

It might be helpful at some point for you to hear those familiar tones again.

But you might also want to gather your memories in a journal. These memories will fade over time, so it might be nice to jot them down as you remember them.

Is this too much focusing on the past? Not really. Oh, it's possible that some might get lost in their backward glances and keep from moving on with their lives. But isn't that what the grieving process is all about—looking back, looking forward, remembering the past, giving it a place of honor, and then stepping into the future?

June Cerza Kolf tells another story of a woman named Lynn who was grieving her father's death. He and Lynn's mom were preparing to move. All their things were boxed up, in storage, when he passed away suddenly. It was months later when Lynn finally helped her mother move. There were the boxes, lovingly packed by the now-departed father. Lynn feared that each one would have heartbreaking memories and that opening them would be a difficult ordeal. But she decided to look for the laughter along with the tears.

"Mom, remember when Dad and I used to bring you breakfast in bed and we used this coffee server? We would giggle as we tried to work quietly in the kitchen so you would be surprised. And this baseball—how Daddy liked to toss it to our puppy!"

Kolf describes it as a choice of laughter over tears. Lynn was deciding how to handle her memories, and you will have similar choices. There's nothing wrong with tears. Some of your memories will rip your heart out. You'll cry all night, and that's fine. Yet, increasingly, you'll be able to smile and even laugh over old memories and hold them in your heart as you face the days ahead.

Chapter 14

# Times of Hope

***It is a gift of God. Through the haze of hurt, we get hints of happiness. We begin to see that a new life is ahead of us.***

For surely I know the plans I have for you, says the Lord, plans for your welfare and not for harm, to give you a future with hope.

—Jeremiah 29:11

# After the Grief Subsides

Tara was a strong woman in many ways, but she had never been good at relationships. A miserable failure in her first marriage, she was hesitant to get involved with a new guy. But when she met Kevin, she thought she had a keeper. He was cute and smart and not stuck on himself (as husband number one had been). In fact, he was adorably insecure. He needed her.

Shortly after their engagement, disaster struck. Kevin was diagnosed with a brain disorder. He began a long, slow decline—first mentally and then physically. Tara was determined not to give up on this relationship, as she had the first time. Though she and Kevin weren't married yet, she was as loyal as any wife would be—even when he stopped being the cute guy she fell in love with. He still needed her, and she put aside many of her hopes and dreams in order to care for him.

In a way, she was grieving from the time of the diagnosis. She threw herself into the task of caring for Kevin, and that distracted her from the sorrow, but she knew she would lose him eventually. And she did. Then the floodgates opened. Tara felt a torrent of emotion—anger, deep sorrow, and many questions. Who was she now? A failure at one marriage, a nonstarter at another. She had spent the last few years completely focused on what Kevin wanted and needed as he wasted away. But what did she want? What did she need? Her own personality was wasting away the whole time, and she had never realized it.

For Tara, the tears were spent rather quickly. Since she had been preparing for Kevin's death all along, she didn't need too many months to mourn his passing. But what she desperately needed was what the experts call reorganization and reinvestment. She had to discover a new world in which she could participate fully, not as a nursemaid to someone else, but as a . . . as a what? She didn't even know.

Fortunately for Tara, she had caring friends who helped her through this discovery process.

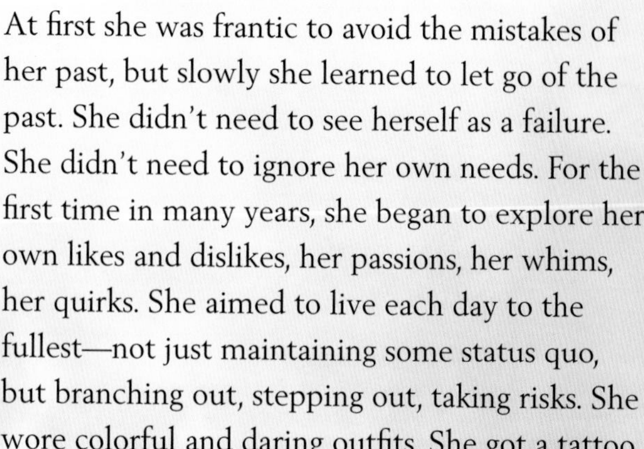

At first she was frantic to avoid the mistakes of her past, but slowly she learned to let go of the past. She didn't need to see herself as a failure. She didn't need to ignore her own needs. For the first time in many years, she began to explore her own likes and dislikes, her passions, her whims, her quirks. She aimed to live each day to the fullest—not just maintaining some status quo, but branching out, stepping out, taking risks. She wore colorful and daring outfits. She got a tattoo.

The tattoo freaked out her very conservative mother. In fact, both parents were really concerned about Tara. Her self-discovery seemed more troubling than her grieving had been. But she was learning to take care of herself, not to please everyone else. This might sound selfish on her part, and that's what her parents were charging, but it was actually a step toward personal wholeness. She was still the sweet, caring woman she had always been, but now she was mining the core of her identity. Where did that sweetness come from? A desire to prove her value to society or an expression of love from a healthy heart?

There was also a spiritual restoration in this process. For several years, Tara had rejected the strict faith of her parents, though she wasn't telling them that. The painful experience with Kevin just didn't fit into the categories she had been taught. Yes, she was angry with God, and though she still stopped into church occasionally, it was just for show.

But as she began to examine her heart, she came to realize that she really did have faith, deep in her core. It wasn't founded on rules and expectations, but on the love of God. This God wasn't high and distant, dispensing judgment and "I told you so." Tara realized that God was a sufferer himself, used to rejection, "acquainted with grief." Tara had some Christian friends who nurtured her rediscovery of faith.

**Hope. Heaven's own gift to struggling mortals; pervading, like some subtle essence from the skies, all things, both good and bad; as universal as death, and more infectious than disease!**

**—Charles Dickens, *Nicholas Nickleby***

The tears over Kevin had generally stopped. Oh, there were reminders from time to time, wistful memories from their early days, but Tara's grieving process was no longer about him. It was about her. And over the year following Kevin's death, she slowly reassembled her own sense of self. This was her healing. This was her hope for the future.

It's not unusual for the grieving process to turn a corner in its final stages. It stops looking backward and starts looking forward. It's less about the one you've lost and more about *you*. You might feel a little guilty about this change, but there's no need for that. This is an important shift, necessary for your healing process. What's more, it's exactly what your loved one would want you to do.

The questions now: *Who are you? How will you move forward? On what basis can you find hope for the future?*

*I am confident of this, that the one who began a good work among you will bring it to completion by the day of Jesus Christ.*

—Philippians 1:6

# A Future with Hope

Jeremiah is known as "the weeping prophet." He had bad news for the nation of Judah. They would be conquered by an enemy country, and many of their citizens would be taken captive. He predicted 70 years of captivity.

Of course, the people didn't want to hear it, so Jeremiah proclaimed his prophecy louder and stronger. The nation was in for a bad time ahead. They could try to deny that fact, but it would happen nonetheless.

Yet this prophet's message was not all gloom and doom. The time of captivity would eventually end, and God would restore his people. In the scripture that leads off this chapter, the Lord discusses his "plans." He would give them a "future with hope."

There's a similarity between Jeremiah's message and the message of this book. As you work through the grief of losing a loved one, things will get worse before they get better. But they will get better.

It might be the furthest thing from your mind right now, but you will be happy again. That doesn't mean you'll forget about the one you've lost—far from it. You will treasure their memory, thankful for the time you had together. But your life will go on. You will try some new things. You will develop other relationships. You will discover new strength of character. You will find surprising new ways to help other people. And you will have a more resilient relationship with God.

**Grief, O God of current and tides, is taking me somewhere new. Feeling your guiding hand, I will hold on and keep moving.**

Listen to what the Lord said through the prophet Jeremiah: "I will fulfill to you my promise and bring you back to this place. For surely I know the plans I have for you, says the Lord, plans for your welfare and not for harm, to give you a future with hope. Then when you call upon me and come and pray to me, I will hear you. When you search for me, you will find me; if you seek me with all your heart, I will let you find me, says the Lord, and I will restore your fortunes" (Jeremiah 29:10–14).

It's clear that the Lord wants to be close to you. He knows what you're going through. He understands that your relationship with him might be a bit rocky right now. But it won't always be that way. He will help you sort through your expectations and assumptions about him, and he'll work with you to build a new way of interacting, based on the reality of who he is. Despite your questions and doubts—no, actually *because* of your questions and doubts—the Lord will be a powerful force in your life.

A future with hope. That's what I long for.
Tomorrows that teem with adventure.
After my desolate winter of grief,
hope springs eternal for me.
You've guided me through the long
pathway of healing,
salved me and saved me and
satisfied longings.
Now I see visions of glory ahead,
a future of purpose and joy.
Lead me on, my King, my Healer.
Unfold the life that remains.
Let my existence bring praise to you always.
May others grow strong through my pain.
Hope is about believing with a
humble heart that tomorrow can
be different. It's about knowing that light will
come to chase away this darkness.

# Living with Hope

In the throes of depression, you get nearsighted. That is, you start looking only at this day, this room, this problem. You're not thinking about the wider world. You have little sense of the future. You just want to get through the day. If you're functioning at all, you are plodding rather than walking—certainly not dancing.

As the depression lifts, your sight changes. No, not the strength of your glasses, but the way you see your life. You begin to look at larger issues. You begin to think about your future. You even begin to hope.

In fact, hope might be the key word for that change. Hopelessness turns to hopefulness. For the first time in a year or so, things are beginning to look up.

With hope, then, comes the courage to step out of your protective shell. Maybe you learn to love again (not necessarily in a romantic way, but at least in the form of a solid new friendship). Maybe you start thinking again about your goals in life. You've just come face-to-face with death; what do you want to accomplish in the time you have left? Maybe there's some new ministry you want to launch or join. Maybe some cause you can support. Can you pass your wisdom on to a new generation by teaching Sunday school? Can you reach out to less fortunate folks by working in a soup kitchen? Can you raise money for research to fight the disease that took your loved one?

**If time is a great healer, then love is the caring aide who works side by side, hand in hand with time to heal our pain and bring us back to the living.**

Hope allows you to look forward rather than backward. Instead of mourning what you have lost from the past, you can use your past experiences to propel you into the future with hope. And, having gone through deep grief, you have battle-tested your emotions. You can take some new chances because you're not as fragile as you used to be.

# God's Great Faithfulness

Are you ready to move forward in hope? Maybe not. You might still be working through the process. If that's the case, dog-ear these pages and come back to them later. Hope will be there for you when you're ready. And maybe just knowing that will help you get through some difficult days.

Jeremiah did that sort of thing. He knew all about the hopeful future God had promised, but it was still tough to see his nation ravished. The book of Lamentations records his reaction to the destruction of Jerusalem, something he had warned about, but people didn't want to hear his message.

"He has filled me with bitterness, he has sated me with wormwood. He has made my teeth grind on gravel, and made me cower in ashes; my soul is bereft of peace; I have forgotten what happiness is; so I say, 'Gone is my glory, and all that I had hoped for from the Lord' " (Lamentations 3:15–18).

Maybe you've been there. Happiness is a distant memory. Jeremiah describes his feelings in very bitter terms. His soul is "bowed down" within him.

Then he turns a corner. "But this I call to mind, and therefore I have hope: The steadfast love of the Lord never ceases, his mercies never come to an end; they are new every morning; great is your faithfulness" (vs. 21–23).

The prophet has been describing the destruction of his city. Still he hails the steadfast love of the Lord. God's mercies are brand new day after day after day.

He goes on to declare that the Lord is his "portion." God is enough. "Therefore I will hope in him" (v. 24).

There's that word again. Hope. Shelve it for the future maybe, but don't forget it. Claim it. Use it. Let it propel you into a glorious future.

*Lord of yesterday, today, and tomorrow, I now see that you've been with me all along. Even in those challenging times, you were holding me tight.*

*I understand that you're with me right now. When I need a word to say, you supply it. When I need comfort, you soothe my soul.*

*And now I need to trust you with my future. Where is all of this going? What's ahead for me? Only you can know that.*

*I don't know what the future holds, but I know you hold the future. Amen.*

It is you who light my lamp;
the Lord, my God, lights up my darkness.

—Psalm 18:28

The Lord is good to those who wait for him, to the soul that seeks him. It is good that one should wait quietly for the salvation of the Lord.

—Lamentations 3:25–26

*God, your love moves mountains; please now move a mountain of grief from my path. Your grace creates miracles; please send me a miracle of newfound joy in a life that right now holds no happiness. Your power heals the sick at heart; please comfort me with a soothing balm that calms and nourishes my dried-up soul. God, pour yourself upon me like the rain that brings new life to a dry earth. Amen.*

# A New You

The question for you now is this: *What kind of person will you be, say, a year from now?* We'll give you that lead time to make sure you've recovered from your grief. We'll assume that, a year from now, you've gotten back to some kind of equilibrium emotionally. Oh, you will certainly miss the one you've lost, but you'll be dealing with that loss. You'll be looking forward rather than backward.

So, who will you be—in your heart and soul, in your priorities and relationships? Is there a "new you" that will emerge from this grief? That's not as mystical as it sounds. We are constantly remaking ourselves, aren't we? You were a different person ten years ago than you are now, and you were even more different five years before that. Yet, when a crisis occurs—like the loss of someone very close to us—we tend to make greater changes. Think about it: The momentous events of your life, good or bad, have shaped you more than anything else.

So, as you emerge from this crisis, what is the new shape of you?

Before we dig further, let's deal with a potential pitfall. You might be apt to define this "new you" according to the desires and dreams of the person you've lost. Say, your mother always wanted you to be a doctor so now, after her death, you'll apply to medical school. That's not necessarily the right move. (But it's not necessarily the wrong move either.)

We're still dealing with *you*—your hopes and dreams, your abilities, your fulfillment. In some cases, those departed loved ones might have longed for you to fulfill your squandered potential, and so you might use this loss as a propellant to get your life on track. In other cases, to be brutally honest, they sought to nag, manipulate, and control you while they were alive. Don't let them do this to you from the grave. This is your life now. If their memory inspires you, use that. But transform their hopes and dreams into something that you can live with. You honor their memory more by using your God-given qualities in a way that fits *you*.

So, back to the question: *What kind of YOU will you be?*

Think about your *priorities.* Has this encounter with mortality made you more aware of eternity? Has that challenged your notion of what's most important in life? One wealthy man did a radical purge of his lifestyle after his wife died. "I had everything I ever wanted, except happiness," he explained. "And my wealth was keeping me from being happy." His grief had forced him to take a hard look at his priorities. For you, it might be a matter of how many hours you work, or how much effort you put into relationships, or how you're using your creative gifts. Your current crisis might convince you to make important changes to invest your life in what matters most.

Think about your *relationships.* Will you be reluctant to open your heart again, after suffering this loss? Maybe for a while. But your personal pain might open you up to new pos-

sibilities. There are all sorts of hurting people in this world who are routinely avoided by the general public. Has your painful experience prepared you to connect with others who are in pain? Will your new identity be one characterized by understanding, compassion, and mercy? Will you be more humble in your relationships, now that you have questioned everything you thought you knew? Has the challenge to your belief system made you more tolerant of those who believe differently?

Think about your *emotional life.* Is it any easier to cry now, or to laugh? If you've always been careful with emotional displays, have you now learned to express yourself more freely? Will your new identity be one of honest expression?

Think about your *spiritual life.* Chances are, you've been through the wringer with God. You've doubted him, questioned him, scolded him, maybe even hated him for a while. If there were any "graven images" of theological certainty in your life, they've been torn down. Maybe you don't know what you believe anymore. Okay, now spend the next month reading Ruth, Job, the Psalms, Jeremiah, Lamentations, Habakkuk, and Hosea. In all of these writings, people found their ideas of God challenged—and they emerged, at a gut level, with a deeper relationship with God. Their faith grew through doubt. God became more real to them when their old ideas got shattered. So, will that happen to you? What kind of spiritual person will you be, going forward?

Hope turns our vision toward the future. But the question remains: What kind of person will you be when you get there?

*Loving Lord,*

*I pulled open the shade this morning, and the sunshine burst into my room. It seemed to burst into my life. I've been wearing blinders for months now, closing my eyes to the radiant existence you're offering.*

*But now I think I'm ready. Lead me forward into the life you want for me. Give me the wisdom I need, the courage I need, the character I need to honor you as I take these next steps.*

*I trust you for all this. Amen.*

*Conclusion*

# Moving Forward

***What do you do when you're emotionally ready to get on with your life? How do you re-enter civilization after you've taken a much-needed break?***

You have turned my mourning into dancing; you have taken off my sackcloth and clothed me with joy, so that my soul may praise you and not be silent. O Lord my God, I will give thanks to you forever.

—Psalm 30:11–12

# Getting on with Life

It was a simple question in a church lobby. "Do you have a widows' group in this church? I lost my husband a year-and-a-half ago, and I'm ready to get back into life again." The woman had gotten up the gumption to go out visiting churches, and she had found one she liked. Now if only she could find people who understood her, people who had been where she had.

She was directed to a singles group where she would find a number of people who had lost their mates, people who were eager to move forward with their lives.

How about you? Are you ready to move forward?

It's okay if you're not. If you've learned one thing from this book, it might be that there's no clock to punch in grief recovery. You don't have a set schedule. There are so many complex factors involved in each person's process, it's impossible to define a time frame that works for everybody. Various experts have defined some stages of grief, and these can be a sort of road map if you want it. Still, they keep adding new stages, so it's hard to keep track of where you are at any point.

It sounds a little wishy-washy to say that your pathway is yours alone. But it's true. You will go through whatever stages you need to go through for as long as you need to go through them. You may bounce back and forth through the chapters of this book—"Times of Anger," then "Times of Deep Sorrow," then back to "Anger," then some "Times of Discouragement." It can be a wild ride.

**He has sent me to . . . bind up the brokenhearted.**
**—Isaiah 61:1**

But then you start being "ready to get back into life again." Since you've gotten this far in this book, you might be ready already, or you soon will be.

What will "moving forward" mean for you?

For one thing, it means finding a good place in your heart for your grief. The sorrow doesn't go away entirely. The memories are still there. You will always miss this person you have loved so dearly. But through the grief process, you have paid a kind of debt, and now you can tuck that grief away, somewhere inside you. You'll take it out for special occasions and grieve again (a little or sometimes a lot). But in general, you'll go on with your life, changed forever by the love you've had, but no longer held back by it.

It means developing new friendships, taking the risk of sharing yourself with others, knowing that there might be more pain ahead. Perhaps you will find like-minded souls—a support group or a widows' group or just a really great Bible study group where you can open your soul and invite people in.

It means honoring your lost loved one with your life. You have already honored them with your tears; now it's time to live a life worthy of their love. Not that you have to do everything they would have wanted. Even when they were alive, they didn't always know what was best for you. Instead, pour your energy into the act of living, and let that be a fitting memorial.

*The Lord is my light and my salvation; whom shall I fear? The Lord is the stronghold of my life; of whom shall I be afraid? . . . For he will hide me in his shelter in the day of trouble; he will conceal me under the cover of his tent; he will set me high on a rock. . . . I believe that I shall see the goodness of the Lord in the land of the living. Wait for the Lord; be strong, and let your heart take courage; wait for the Lord!*

—Psalm 27:1, 5, 13–14

*Then shall the young women rejoice in the dance, and the young men and the old shall be merry. I will turn their mourning into joy, I will comfort them, and give them gladness for sorrow.*

—Jeremiah 31:13

# Three Widows

The biblical book of Ruth shows us three bereaved women at this point of moving forward. The backstory is simple. Naomi and her husband were Israelites who migrated in a time of famine to the neighboring nation of Moab. They had two sons who grew up and married Moabite girls. First Naomi's husband died. Then the two sons died. Naomi was left with her two daughters-in-law, Ruth and Orpah.

Naomi decided to return to Israel, to her extended family, and she urged the younger women to go back to their original homes in Moab. Orpah did so, but Ruth didn't. That's why she got a book written about her.

She was a grieving young widow. She had lost the love of her life, and her economic outlook was dim. It probably would have made sense to retreat to her parents' home, to find someone in her clan who would take her in, but Ruth took advantage of this opportunity to examine who she was and what was most important. This is what she said:

*Do not press me to leave you*
*or to turn back from following you!*
*Where you go, I will go;*
*where you lodge, I will lodge;*
*your people shall be my people,*
*and your God my God.*
*Where you die, I will die—*
*there will I be buried.*
*May the Lord do thus and so to me,*
*and more as well,*
*if even death parts me from you!*

—Ruth 1:16–17

You might have heard this read, in some form, at a wedding. It is indeed a beautiful expression of love and commitment. People might be surprised to learn that it was first said by a young woman to her mother-in-law.

Apparently Ruth had found something valuable in Naomi, in Naomi's people, and in Naomi's faith. She was not about to let that go. She was saying, *I will no longer be the person I used to be. I will be part of Naomi's people now.*

The rest of the story is pretty good too. Life is hard for these two women, but it gets better.

Largely through Naomi's coaching, Ruth finds a new husband, and that makes everything better. But here's a detail you might miss. Ruth and her new husband have a child, who later becomes the grandfather of King David, who was of course an ancestor of Jesus. Matthew boldly includes Ruth, this foreign woman, in his genealogy of Jesus.

So, let's get this straight. Because the grieving Ruth decided to move forward as she did, committing herself to Naomi's people and to her faith, she had a significant part in the most important event that ever happened in the history of the world.

Not to put any pressure on you, but you'll be making some decisions as you "get back into life." The very woes you have suffered have prepared you for these decisions. They have pruned you. They have strengthened you.

One more thing. You are now uniquely prepared to help others who are suffering. As you step back into the game, look for opportunities to help sufferers. Because of your own suffering, you can help them in a way no one else can.

*Lord,*

*You're asking me to dance? You must not understand. I've been in mourning. I've suffered a great loss. How can you expect me to turn mourning into dancing? I don't see how that's possible. I haven't danced in so long. There must be more grieving to do.*

*Please, not yet. I'm not ready, am I? I've never been very good on my feet, but now you're leading me out onto the dance floor. How can I resist?*

*Lord, watch me dance. This is for you, dear Lord.*

In the depth of winter, I finally learned that within me there lay an invincible summer.

—Albert Camus

*You need not cry very loud:*
*he is nearer to us than we think.*

—Brother Lawrence

*Let nothing disturb thee;*
*Let nothing dismay thee;*
*All things pass;*
*God never changes.*
*Patience attains*
*All this it strives for.*
*He who has God*
*Finds he lacks nothing.*
*God alone suffices.*

—St. Teresa of Avila

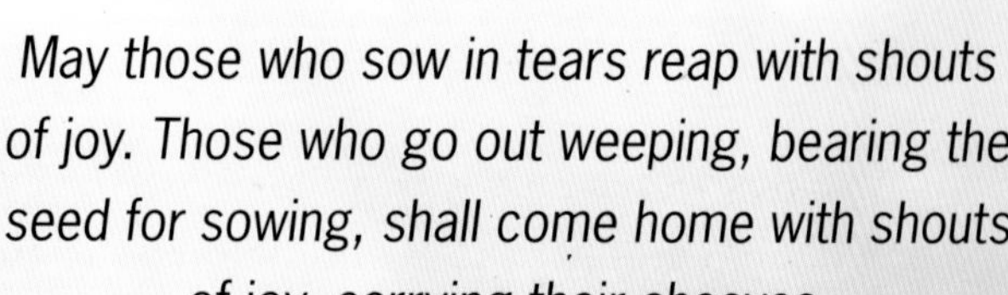

*May those who sow in tears reap with shouts of joy. Those who go out weeping, bearing the seed for sowing, shall come home with shouts of joy, carrying their sheaves.*

—Psalm 126:5–6

*For my part,*
*I will sing of your strength;*
*I will celebrate your love*
*in the morning; For you have*
*become my stronghold,*
*a refuge in the day*
*of my trouble.*
*To you, O my Strength, will I sing;*
*for you, O God, are my stronghold*
*and my merciful God.*

—*The Book of Common Prayer*, Church of England

# Bible Verse Guide

The Bible has words to inspire, comfort, and guide you. This index will help you know what Bible verses to turn to in times of need or crisis.

**Anger**
Psalm 4:4
Psalm 37:8
Proverbs 14:17
Proverbs 15:1
Proverbs 22:24–25
Proverbs 27:4
Ecclesiastes 7:9
Matthew 5:22
Ephesians 4:26, 31–32
1 Timothy 2:8

**Death**
Psalm 33:18–19
John 3:16
Romans 6:23
1 Corinthians 15:51–52
2 Corinthians 5:1–4
Philippians 1:20–24
Hebrews 2:14–15
Revelation 2:11

**Depression**
Job 3
Psalm 6:8–10
Psalm 30:10–12
Psalm 31:12–14
Psalm 42:9–11
Psalm 56:8–11
Psalm 94:17–19
Proverbs 14:13
Ecclesiastes 7:3–5
2 Corinthians 1:3–5

**Discouragement**
Joshua 1:6–9
Esther 4:13–16
Isaiah 1:17
Romans 1:11–12
Colossians 2:1–3
1 Thessalonians 5:11–14
Hebrews 3:13
Hebrews 10:25

**Fear**
Psalm 23:4
Psalm 27:1
Isaiah 41:10

Luke 12:4–5
Philippians 2:12
2 Timothy 1:7

**Illness**
Psalm 41:4
Psalm 107:19–20
Psalm 147:3
Isaiah 53:5
Isaiah 58:8
Jeremiah 33:6
Malachi 4:2
Matthew 8:16–17
John 4:46–53
James 5:14–16

**Indecision**
Psalm 27:13
Isaiah 33:6
Romans 8:33–39
Ephesians 1:4–5
Philippians 1:6
1 Thessalonians 1:4–5
Hebrews 10:19–23
Hebrews 11:1
1 John 5:13

**Repentance**
1 Samuel 7:3
Ezekiel 18:31–32
Matthew 3:1–8
Matthew 4:17
Luke 15:7, 10
Luke 19:8–9
Acts 2:37–39
Acts 3:19–20
Acts 8:22–24
Romans 2:4
2 Peter 3:9

**Suffering**
Book of Job
Psalm 43:2–3
Psalm 50:15
Psalm 107:26–31
Psalm 112:4–8
Psalm 119:71
Romans 5:3–5
2 Corinthians 1:5–11
Hebrews 10:32–35
1 Peter 2:19–21

**Worry**
Psalm 94:19
Psalm 139:23
Ecclesiastes 2:22–24
Matthew 6:25–34
Matthew 10:19–20
Philippians 4:6
1 Peter 5:7